Product-Line Performance Evaluation Systems *for* Financial Depositories

Kenneth J. Thygerson

Quorum Books
Westport, Connecticut • London

332.10688
T54p

Library of Congress Cataloging-in-Publication Data

Thygerson, Kenneth J. (Kenneth James)
  Product-line performance evaluation systems for financial
depositories / by Kenneth J. Thygerson.
    p.   cm.
  Includes bibliographical references and index.
  ISBN 1–56720–104–0 (alk. paper)
  1. Bank marketing—United States—Evaluation.   2. Financial
services industry—United States—Evaluation.   3. Financial services
industry—United States—Marketing.   4. Financial engineering—
United States.   I. Title.
HG1616.M3T49   1997
332.1′068′8—dc20   96–32509

British Library Cataloguing in Publication Data is available.

Library of Congress Catalog Card Number: 96–32509
ISBN: 1–56720–104–0

First published in 1997

Quorum Books, 88 Post Road West, Westport, CT 06881
An imprint of Greenwood Publishing Group, Inc.

Printed in the United States of America

The paper used in this book complies with the
Permanent Paper Standard issued by the National
Information Standards Organization (Z39.48–1984).

10 9 8 7 6 5 4 3 2 1

To Keith and Kent

Contents

Illustrations   ix

Preface   xiii

Chapter 1: The Changing Competitive Environment Facing   1
Depositories

Chapter 2: Why New Product-Line Performance Measures Are   5
Needed

Chapter 3: Unbundling the Functions of Financial Depositories   15

Chapter 4: The Basics of Product-Line Performance Measurement   35

Chapter 5: Traditional Measures of Depository Performance: 47
Strengths and Weaknesses

Chapter 6: Noninterest Income Sources (Origination, Servicing, and 73
Brokerage Revenue)

Chapter 7: Product-Line Performance Appraisal Systems   85
Introduction

Chapter 8: Measuring Retail Depository Branch Performance   97

Chapter 9: Measuring Loan Origination Office Performance   113

Chapter 10: Managing the Performance Measure Implementation   119
Process

Chapter 11: Measuring Performance of Local Promotion and   129
Advertising Programs

Contents

Chapter 12: Cost Cutting with Product-Line Systems   137

Selected Bibliography   143

Index   145

Illustrations

EXHIBITS

1.1 Stages of Strategy Development   3

3.1 Origination Function   22

3.2 Servicing Functions   23

3.3 Brokerage Function   24

3.4 Organization Chart for 1st National Bank   30

8.1 FDIC-Insured Banks and Offices 1959–1993   98

10.1 Organizational Staffing and Reporting Relationships   121

11.1 Return on Promotion Investment   133

11.2 Promotion Plan   134

11.3 Promotion Timeline Report   136

TABLES

2.1 Credit Card Profit-and-Loss Statement   11

3.1 Financial Claim/Function Matrix for Assets   26

3.2 Financial Claim/Function Matrix for Liabilities   28

3.3 1st National Bank of Williamsport, South Carolina Balance   29
Sheet for December 31, 1996

3.4 Financial Claim/Function Matrix for Assets and Liabilities 1st National Bank of Porter, Indiana 31

3.5 Common Origination and Servicing Functions of Depositories 31

4.1 Fully Allocated Profitability Model for Auto Lending Department 38

4.2 Marginal Contribution Expense Approach for Auto Lending Department 40

4.3 Customer Profitability Model 42

4.4 Product and Process Profitability Performance Statement 43

5.1 Time-Series Analysis Percent Return on Beginning-of-the-Year Equity for First Bank: Quarterly 1995–1996 49

5.2 Cross-Sectional Financial Ratio Analysis of First Bank and Two Competitors 49

5.3 Time-Series Analysis Percent Return on Beginning-of-the-Year Equity for First Bank and Peer Group: Quarterly 1995–1996 49

5.4a First Bank Common-Size Income Statement and Supplemental Data 50

5.4b Common-Size Balance Sheet and Supplemental Data 50

5.5 Net Interest Margin, Net Interest Spread, and Net Interest Spread to Average Assets 1996 56

5.6 Selected Profit Performance Measures for All Commercial Banks 1990–1995 57

5.7 Asset Quality Trends at Commercial Banks 1990–1994 62

5.8 Noninterest Expense to Total Assets at All Commercial Banks, 1990–1994 69

6.1 Net Interest Income and Noninterest Income for Insured Commercial Banks 1989–1995 75

6.2 Noninterest Income as a Percent of Earning Assets by Size of Bank: 1994 76

6.3 Noninterest Income and Expenses as a Percent of Earning Assets for Different Sized Commercial Banks in 1994 78

7.1 Annual Pro-Forma Income Statement for XYZ Bank In-House Mortgage Origination Unit 88

7.2 Product-Line Statement for In-House Servicing Unit 90

7.3 XYZ Commercial Bank Income Statement 92

7.4 Product-Line Income and Expense Statement   94

7.5 Estimated Return on Equity for Functions Performed by XYZ   95
Commercial Bank

8.1 Example of Deposit Cost Comparisons for All Deposits Sold by   104
a Branch in One Month

8.2 Present Value of Interest Savings Calculated at the Firm's   105
Weighted Cost of Capital (9.00%) for All Deposits Rolled Over and
New Deposits Received for the Month of July 1996

8.3 Schedule of Fee and Commission Income for a One-Month   106
Period (*BFC*)

8.4 Monthly Direct and Indirect Costs of Operating a Retail Branch   106
(*BTC*)

8.5 Monthly Income Statement for Hypothetical Branch (*TBP*)   107

8.6 Estimated Deposit Balances and Average Spread Compared to   110
Wholesale Funding Source for 1993–1996 and Beyond

8.7 Account Servicing and Conversion Costs   111

8.8 Investment Analysis   112

9.1 Mortgage Originator's Revenue   116

9.2 Income Statement for Mortgage Origination Unit   116

10.1 Classification Approaches to Indirect Cost Allocations   123

FIGURE

2.1 Economies of Scale   12

Preface

This book is the product of over ten years of on-the-job effort to develop performance measures for the financial depository industry. These efforts involved a team of financial and economic experts who worked for a large financial services company. Over a period of several years, product-line performance systems were designed, tested, and implemented for each operating unit within the firm. These systems have subsequently been implemented in a number of other financial depositories.

The test of any performance system is how well it affects behavior. The systems described in this volume have a profound impact on the behavior of managers throughout depositories. Using the systems, managers of profit centers involved in origination, servicing, and brokerage are better able to focus on only those business factors over which they have control and which truly affect the profitability of their businesses. Staff support units are similarly affected since they must justify their costs which are allocated to profit centers. Deposit-gathering branch managers are motivated by their performance system, which focuses on selling financial products and services and allows them to easily track their success daily, if desired, and respond quickly to market opportunities. They also enjoy the opportunity to plan and execute product promotions using the promotion and advertising performance system included in this book.

All the systems discussed are based on theoretically proven models of the functions of financial institutions. Some of the material in this book has been previously published. The chapters on financial functions and on noninterest expenses were modified from chapters in *Management of Financial Institutions* (Thygerson, HarperCollins College Publishers, 1995). A version of the deposit branch model was published in the *Journal of Retail Banking* (Thygerson, 1991). A version of the product-line profitability model was published in *The*

Community Banker (Thygerson, 1995). The book has substantially expanded on these previous efforts.

A number of people have contributed considerably to the development of the performance systems described in this book. Dr. Kevin Villani, CFO of Imperial Credit Industries and Clinical Professor of Finance at the University of Southern California, and Dr. Michael Lea, principal of Cardiff Consulting and instructor at the University of California, San Diego, were instrumental in the early development and implementation of these systems. Without their pioneering efforts, the book would not be possible.

Chapter 1 ....

The Changing Competitive Environment Facing Depositories

Every facet of the financial services business has become more competitive. Financial markets first became national and now international. The internet promises to make the delivery of financial services available to every person on the face of the earth who owns a phone. Nonbanks have carved out huge segments of the traditional markets once serviced exclusively by depositories. As recently as 1980, price controls on savings and time deposits protected the profit margins of many depositories. No longer. This protected market has been replaced by a $2.6 trillion mutual fund industry that offers consumers and businesses virtually every combination of risk and return on investments selected from markets worldwide.

Federal government-sponsored enterprises like Fannie Mae and Freddie Mac dominate pricing in the home mortgage market. Sallie Mae attempted to dominate the student loan market. Investment bankers first served high-grade corporate customers through the consumer paper market in the early 1970s and then noninvestment-grade borrowers with the junk bond in the 1980s. This leaves few underserved business loan markets for commercial banks.

Making matters worse, the transaction account market, once the sole domain of commercial banks, is now shared with thousands of thrift institutions and nonbanks. Commercial and industrial firms are now numbered among the largest credit card issuers in the nation. Even worse, electronic money is making inroads. The internet has several providers of cybernet money already being used. Microsoft Corp. and others have their eyes on the potential for bill paying and other services for the cybernet market.

With so few underserved markets for depositories, the only viable strategy for many is to give it up and be acquired. Others find that downsizing and shrinkage is a reasonable strategy. Even record profits in the 1993-1995 period for commercial banks have not eliminated the need for cost cutting. This is because the major improvements in profits are arising largely from reduced money costs and lower credit losses, not from growing revenue stemming from expanding markets.

For savings and loans and savings banks, the situation has been even more difficult. Thrifts insured by the Savings and Loan Insurance Fund (SAIF) dropped in number from 2,177 in 1991 to 1,773 on June 30, 1995. Their total assets have declined by over $400 billion during this period. The level of reserves held in the SAIF is well below that of the Bank Insurance Fund, causing Congress to propose merging the two funds and eliminating the federal savings and loan and savings bank charters altogether.

All this puts enormous pressure on managers and directors of depositories to find new strategies to improve financial performance. Developing a new strategy is a three-step process as shown in Exhibit 1.1. Step 1 is to clearly define the existing business functions of the firm. Step 2 is to use improved performance systems and data to measure the performance of each product line as they now operate. These performance measures should identify which product lines are currently being performed efficiently and profitably and which are not. Step 3 is to make the necessary changes in personnel and operations or, if necessary, changes in the mix of product lines and activities performed by the firm to improve overall performance.

The most difficult step in this process is step 2—obtaining correct measures of performance of each product-line unit within the firm. These measures are particularly difficult to develop for financial depositories because the various functions of the firm are rarely clearly or properly delineated. Adding to the problem is the fact that under Generally Accepted Accounting Principles (GAAP), the revenues and costs of depositories are not categorized to conform to the different product-line functions performed. This means it is necessary to develop new management accounting reports that reclassify the revenues and costs of the firm to conform to these product lines.

The purpose of this book is to develop theoretically sound and practical systems for unbundling the product-line functions of each depository. These systems will permit each operating unit to identify those revenues and costs of the firm over which they have accountability.

Using this process, several performance systems are developed which allow management to measure the performance of each functional operating unit and branch office.

Chapter 2 provides a discussion of why product-line performance measures are needed to improve the management of financial depositories.

Chapter 3 provides a structure for defining each of the various products and services created by depositories and the functions performed in the process. One objective of the chapter is the development of a "financial claim/function matrix," which is used to delineate each product and service and the functions performed to deliver each one.

Chapter 4 provides basic information about how performance measure systems are developed. Included is a discussion of how to allocate costs among the various operating units of the firm. The chapter also explains various alternative performance measurement systems used in the industry and explains which ones are best suited for depositories.

Exhibit 1.1
Stages of Strategy Development

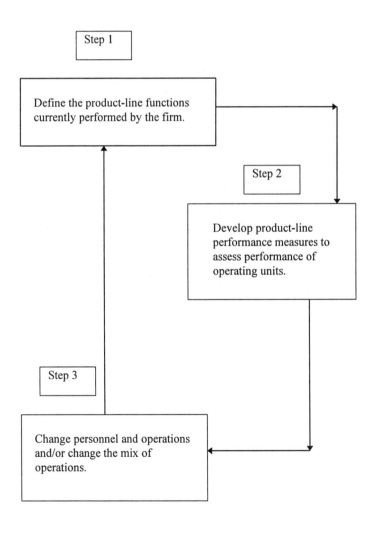

Chapter 5 provides an in-depth discussion of the traditional measures of depository performance. The chapter focuses on global measures of performance and those that are especially useful for assessing the performance of the firm's investment portfolio managers.

Chapter 6 provides a discussion of noninterest sources of depository revenue. It focuses on those income sources related to origination, servicing, and brokerage product-line functions performed by the firm.

Chapter 7 provides generalized product-line performance appraisal systems for depositories. These systems are especially suited for specialized units within the firm involved in origination, servicing, and brokerage activities.

Chapter 8 provides a specialized performance system of the deposit-gathering branches of depositories. It provides a methodology for assessing the value added of the retail deposits attracted into retail branches. It also explains how to use the system to evaluate bank deposit-gathering branch purchases, sales, and swaps.

Chapter 9 provides a specialized performance model of the loan origination offices of depositories. Depositories large enough to have business loan and mortgage origination offices can use this model to assess the performance of the origination functions performed by the staff of these offices.

Chapter 10 explains the management organization issues involved in implementing the performance measurement systems. The chapter explains the creation of a development task forces, the tasks to be accomplished, and the problems that must be resolved.

Chapter 11 provides a performance measurement system for executing advertising and promotions at the local branch level. This system has been successfully used to delegate certain advertising and promotion budgets to branches so that they can be used to promote the firm at the local level and still hold the staff implementing the program accountable for the funds expended.

Chapter 12 explains how to use the performance systems introduced in this book to set corporate priorities and cut out unnecessary expenses.

Chapter 2 ....

Why New Product-Line Performance Measures Are Needed

INTRODUCTION

Specialists dominate the financial landscape today. Gone are the days when many financial depositories could attempt to be full service financial department stores offering many products in hopes that customers would buy a few of the firm's most profitable products. Today, every financial product offered faces stiff competition. Twenty years ago most medium- and large-sized commercial banks offered their own credit card. Over the years, however, the cost advantages of the large-scale issuers all but drove the smaller issuers out of the market. Today, many of these smaller firms simply act as agents by brokering cards issued by the big boys. The same is happening in the mortgage origination and servicing businesses.

This trend toward specialization has made it necessary to develop new types of performance measures designed to assess the effectiveness of each product-line function performed by the financial depository. Global measures of institutional performance are still useful, but they do not provide management with the tools it needs to be effective in this age of specialization and intense competition.

THE END OF THE LOSS LEADER

In the pre-1980 days, most depositories could make a list of those products they offered as "loss leaders." The regulation of deposit rates under the Federal Reserve's Regulation Q gave depositories the incentive to provide low-cost or free services to attract depositors. Thrifts gave away everything from toasters to

TVs to attract deposits, while commercial banks countered with free checking accounts, debit cards, and safety deposit boxes. Some consumers fondly remember those days and cannot understand why depositories have to charge for these services today. They do not think about the fact that now depositories pay market rates for savings.

With the end of the loss leader, depositories have had to rethink their firm's product line, pricing strategy, and the role of costly brick-and-mortar branches. Retail branches were a key component of the pre-1980 strategy of giving consumers convenience to offset the lower than market-rate returns offered on savings deposits. Today, many bank mergers, like the mammoth Chase and Chemical Manhattan marriage, are driven by the opportunity to combine branches of two institutions in order to substantially reduce costs and improve on existing economies of scale.

In today's environment, every product and service must carry itself financially or management must have a darn good rationale for why it isn't doing so. This is why it is necessary for management to have performance measures for each product and service offered. Global measures are no longer sufficient to achieve this purpose.

PERFORMANCE SYSTEMS PERMIT ANALYSIS OF OPERATING STRENGTHS AND WEAKNESSES

Product-line performance systems allow management to assess the profit contribution of each division in the firm. Without these systems, it is difficult to assess the performance of all of the many depository operating units. Good product-line performance systems make it possible to determine whether a division offering a particular product, such as auto loans, has one unit able to cover the costs of origination and another unit, charged with servicing the loans, able to do so efficiently. This can't be done using global measures of institutional performance such as return on equity or assets.

Using product-line performance data, management can decide to change the firm's strategy, change prices, withdraw from the market, or expand the activity. With today's active secondary markets for virtually all financial assets and our nation's well developed asset-based security businesses, it is possible for even a small-sized firm to originate and service a volume of loans well beyond its portfolio needs and profit handsomely. However, it is necessary that the firm be especially good at the origination and servicing of these loans. Product-line performance measures allow management to make these assessments.

PERFORMANCE SYSTEMS ANSWER THE QUESTION "DO IT YOURSELF OR SUBCONTRACT?"

Performance measures for each product-line function performed by the depository make it possible to determine whether to do it yourself or subcontract with another firm to obtain origination and servicing services needed. As already mentioned, most depositories have decided it is ineffective to originate and service a credit card portfolio. This highly specialized business is particularly suitable for automation and marketing beyond a single firm's customer base. Consequently, most depositories offer their customers cards with their name on it, but act only as a brokering agent to another specialized card issuer. Others subcontract out data processing and the servicing of demand deposit and other time and savings deposits.

Many institutions find that the secondary market offers the opportunity to diversify their portfolios without having to develop the origination and servicing capabilities to offer the product itself. They can subcontract out the work. A good product-line performance system can help management make the do-it-yourself or subcontract decision.

PERFORMANCE SYSTEMS MAKE IT POSSIBLE TO ASSIGN MANAGEMENT RESPONSIBILITY

One of the most difficult management challenges for a diversified financial depository is establishing accountability and measuring performance of specialized operating units. This is because most traditional measures of depository performance involve mixing a variety of business functions. The unit within the firm responsible for servicing auto loans should not be given incentive programs based broadly on the overall performance of the bank, when the responsibility of the unit is the narrow one of efficiently servicing auto loans. Similarly, a branch manager of a retail branch is not responsible for the net interest margin on the depository's investment portfolio. Therefore, it is usually inappropriate to base this person's compensation and bonus exclusively on the firm's overall portfolio performance.

The objective should be to develop performance measures that relate specifically to the decisions and actions over which each manager has responsibility. The auto loan servicing manager should be evaluated in relation to how efficiently auto loans are serviced in relation to other servicing groups that provide the service.

In the extreme, the depository can always hire an independent firm to service the loans rather than do it in-house. Most branch managers are responsible primarily for attracting retail deposits and providing high quality service to existing customers. Still, many depositories have the alternative to attract funds using wholesale sources including brokered deposits, federal funds, asset-backed securities, and reverse repurchase agreements. As a result, the branch management is effective only if it can bring in deposits at a lower long-term cost. This should be the standard on which performance is evaluated.

The product-line performance measures developed in Chapters 7, 8, and 9 are designed to assign responsibility to managers for only those activities over which they have decision-making responsibility. Each of the performance measures described requires clearly defining the activities of each operating unit and properly determining the revenues and costs associated with each. Once developed, the "do it yourself" or "subcontract out" decision is a simple one.

PERFORMANCE SYSTEMS PERMIT DEVELOPMENT OF COMPENSATION PERFORMANCE SYSTEMS

Once management successfully assigns responsibility to each operating unit, it is possible to create compensation performance programs that unambiguously measure the profit contribution of each unit and compensate each accordingly. The performance measures developed in this book are designed to be used to create such compensation performance programs. These programs allow senior management to monitor performance of each unit within the firm and assign revenue and costs to each in order to determine their profit contribution. This profit-and-loss system becomes the basis for management compensation programs.

PERFORMANCE SYSTEMS CHANGE EMPLOYEE BEHAVIOR

The objective of any performance system is to reinforce good behavior and alter unproductive behavior. Imagine having performance systems that allow each manager to "run his own business." Managers behave differently when they know the sources of the revenue that feed their unit and assume responsibility for the costs they incur. A story will serve to illustrate.

A number of years ago, I participated in a planning meeting for a retail banking unit of a large depository. The unit suffered from high costs, poor customer service, poor morale, and excessive costs both in the branches and in the support units in the home office.

One of our first steps was to interview the product managers who developed, helped price, and supported a growing number of consumer deposit and loan programs. The product managers spent their time in the home office and had little experience in the field. They rarely talked to the branch managers and staff that sold and serviced the programs they created. The meeting's dialog went something like this.

"Bill, you have responsibility for transaction account services don't you?" Mike asked.

"Yes. We offer transaction accounts, credit cards, automated teller services, and direct deposit programs. Our checking program was offered for the first time five years ago. The accounts were offered with no service charges to build market share," Bill responded.

"Tell me, how do we make a profit on an account with no minimum balance when we offer free credit and debit cards and automated teller services?" Mike asked.

Bill responded, "We don't know whether we make a profit or not, but we need to offer the product to provide full service like our competitors."

"Sarah, you're responsible for the retail loan programs offered in the branches, correct?" Mike asked.

"Yes, we offer auto loans, credit cards, home improvement loans, and second mortgages so far," Sarah answered.

"I notice that we only have a few million dollars of each of these loans. How do we make a profit when we factor in the cost of servicing the loans, advertising, and other processing costs?" Mike asked.

"I'm not sure we make a profit or not, but some of our branch personnel believe that the products are needed to be competitive," Sarah commented.

"John, you're responsible for home mortgages, aren't you?" I asked.

"Yes, I am. But we have given up on the branches. We need highly specialized personnel to originate mortgages and the branch staff aren't aggressive enough to compete with mortgage bankers and others. We have set up a mortgage bank subsidiary to do this job with offices located separate from the branches," John responded.

"You mean that we don't use the space in our branches? You go out and lease additional space?" Mike asked.

"Yes." John answered.

Bill spoke up, "I forgot to mention a new product. We just joined a network system that will allow our customers to use ATMs of other financial institutions within our region of the country. This should increase usage of our ATMs and improve customer satisfaction."

"That's interesting. If we're not making a profit on our transaction accounts today, how will we be able to increase our profits by adding a new service that doesn't produce revenue and adds to costs?" Mike asked. "What don't I understand?"

Bill was quick to reply, "I guess all these products and services are really designed to increase our customer base. Then we can sell more of what's really profitable, our savings accounts and certificates of deposit."

"And how profitable are these accounts?" Mike asked. "Our asset/liability committee gets reports which suggest that we pay in the top 20 percent of all competitors in our markets for savings accounts and certificates of deposit."

The question was met with total silence.

The conversation above was held a number of years ago and, hopefully, wouldn't be held today in most depositories. Still, even today, most institutions cannot tell you just how profitable all their products really are. Moreover, the notion that a product can only be justified as a loss leader is still too prevalent on the retail side of the depository business.

This experience serves to highlight the problem of developing clear and consistent incentives that serve stockholder objectives of profitability and return on equity. It's always important to serve the customer. Today, however, it must be done profitably. Some depositors have still not made the transition from the pre-1980 period business strategy of freebies and non-cost-effective loss leaders to profitable cost-effective services. Those firms have found a strategy. Be acquired! The rest will have to develop better systems to manage their bottom line.

PERFORMANCE SYSTEMS ENSURE THE FIRM COVERS ALL ITS COSTS

Shortly after I participated in the above meeting with the product managers, several of them asked for private meetings with me to elaborate on the issues raised by the meeting. One of the meetings was held with the head of the credit card division. She had brought a set of financial reports developed by members of her staff. The meeting went something like the following.

"Mike, can I meet with you for a few minutes? I want to go over the performance of our credit card operation. You see, we *have* financial reports showing just how well we are doing. We know we're making a profit," Sarah opened the meeting.

"Great, I'd like to look at the report [Table 2.1]," Mike responded.

"Does your estimate for average cost of funds include the cost of processing all those deposits?" Mike asked.

"No," Sarah responded.

After reviewing the report, Mike had several additional questions. "Tell me, Sarah, does the credit card division use the services of our centralized data processing group, human resource department, accounting division, legal, and training department? Does it use the branches to solicit cards to our customer base? Does the credit card division pick up any of the costs of executive management and the board of directors?" Mike continued.

"Well, we do get some services from all of them," Sarah responded.

"You didn't include the costs of providing these services on your income statement. You have also included the interest on the credit cards and the cost of funds from the depository. What responsibility do you have for setting the interest rate for the cards, setting deposit rates for the deposits or deciding whether to issue credit-card asset-backed securities to finance the cards?" Mike continued.

"We don't get involved with those matters," Sarah answered.

"What exactly are your people responsible for then?" Mike asked.

"We develop and market our programs through direct mail, through telemarketing, and through the depository's branches. We originate the new accounts. Then we service the existing portfolio and do all the collections work and account rendition," Sarah responded.

"In that case, shouldn't your division be responsible for how efficiently and effectively you implement your solicitation programs and how efficiently you service the portfolio?" Mike asked.

"I suppose so," Sarah answered. "But the books of the firm don't allocate to our division revenue for increasing the number of cards and increasing the credit balances outstanding. We also don't get explicit revenue for the servicing jobs we perform."

"Then we're going to have to develop an accounting system that correctly measures the contributions your division makes to originate and service the accounts," Mike concluded. "In addition, the new system will have to charge your unit for the staff support activities performed for your unit, such as human resources, training, accounting, data processing, and so forth.

Table 2.1
Credit Card Profit-and-Loss Statement
May 199x

Revenue:	
Interest income	$2,500,000
Card fees	90,000
Cash advance fees	100,000
Late fees	3,000
Total revenue	2,690,000
Costs:	
Interest cost (@average cost of funds)	$833,333
Personnel	202,000
Space, heat, light, and telephone	60,000
Membership fees and charges	80,000
Credit losses	625,000
Other costs (e.g., solicitation costs amortized)	100,000
Total costs	$1,900,333
Profit or (loss)	$789,667

"Sarah, thanks for showing your concern. I'll see you at our next staff meeting."

Implementing a robust product-line performance system allows senior management and each operating unit to focus on only those revenue- and cost-generating activities over which the unit has responsibility and avoids agonizing over revenues and costs over which the unit has no control and responsibility.

PERFORMANCE SYSTEMS HELP IDENTIFY ECONOMIES OF SCALE

For years, academics have attempted to prove whether large depositories are inherently more efficient than smaller firms. To the extent that the average cost per unit decreases as volume increases, the firm is said to benefit from economies of scale.[1] For example, if the average cost of servicing mortgages sold in the secondary market fell from $150 per loan to $135 per loan as the total number of loans serviced rose by 15,000, then this would be evidence of economies of scale. If the average cost per unit rises as size (or number of units) increases, the result is diseconomies of scale. Figure 2.1 provides a graphic depiction of the relationship between average cost per dollar of assets for two firms, one benefiting from economies of scale and the other suffering from diseconomies of scale. The line showing economies of scale shows that operating costs per dollar of assets fall as total assets increase, while the opposite occurs for the line showing diseconomies of scale.

Most academic studies have used aggregate data on depository costs and revenues to test for economies of scale. The results of many years of studies are inconclusive. While most analysts believe that very small institutions with assets less than $100 million seem to be less efficient than larger firms, there is no conclusive data on the overall efficiency of firms with assets over $100 million.

Figure 2.1
Economies of Scale

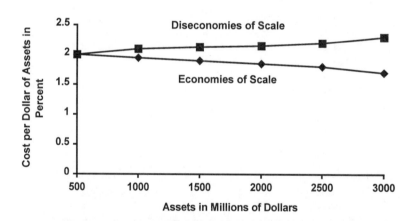

As most managers of financial depositories know full well, it is very hazardous to compare costs between institutions. They differ significantly in terms of the number of different products and services they provide and the functions they perform. A commercial bank with a large mortgage banking origination and servicing unit for loans sold in the secondary market is going to have substantially higher costs per dollar of assets than a firm without this activity. Off-balance sheet activities distort simple measures of operating efficiency and economies of scale. This is certainly the case at very large financial depositories that tend to have large information processing activities involving servicing of loans, security registration, or processing of transactions for other institutions. These off-balance sheet operations are costly to perform, but do not add to the firm's asset base.

Still, the difficulty in measuring economies of scale does not make the concept unimportant. Identifying specific origination and servicing activities that gain from economies of scale, or that suffer from diseconomies, is of critical importance to the long-term strategy of the firm. Those functions that benefit from economies of scale are candidates for expansion, while the reverse may be true for functions with diseconomies of scale.

My experience with financial institution clients suggests that it is easier to obtain economies of scale in the servicing of assets and liabilities than it is in the origination of them. Servicing large portfolios of credit cards, mortgages, transaction accounts, and certificates of deposit all seem to benefit from economies of scale over some large range of increased number of units serviced by the firm. This is because servicing functions readily lend themselves to automation. Many origination functions, however, seem to suffer from diseconomies. This is because the origination of most loans is very labor-intensive. The larger you get, the more layers of supervision and controls are necessary that tend to increase costs.

It is incumbent on management to determine which functions to emphasize and which to deemphasize. The presence, or lack, of economies of scale is an important consideration in this evaluation. Product-line performance systems are very useful to help make these assessments.

SUMMARY

Product-line performance systems are the tools needed in today's competitive atmosphere. These systems allow management to assess the performance of all the operating units within the firm using a theoretically sound approach. Good product-line measures help to change employee behavior to stress profitability, make it easier to develop sound compensation programs, isolate economies of scale, and identify the strong and weak performers within the firm.

NOTE

1. A related concept to economies of scale is economies of scope. This relates to the relationship between per unit costs for products that are produced jointly using the same equipment and personnel. For products jointly produced it is possible to separate costs for each, so they must be evaluated jointly. Interest- and noninterest-paying transaction accounts is an example.

Chapter 3 . . . .

Unbundling the Functions of Financial Depositories

INTRODUCTION

As managers of depositories know only too well, over the years institutional differences among depositories have become less important as legislation and deregulation have allowed financial institutions to offer similar products and serve the same customers. In 1995, Congress began debating a proposal that would eliminate savings and loans and savings banks as distinct institutions. As a result of this melding of powers and authorities, it is more important than ever to focus the resources of the firm on the functions and activities of financial institutions that are relevant to its long-term strategy. Clearly identifying the functions of each depository is the purpose of this chapter.

The identification of the separate functions is referred to as the unbundling of financial services. Unbundling the functions of a depository provides a more useful framework for describing each institution than focusing on the financial institution's aggregate data or its charter type (commercial bank versus thrift). Within each type of financial business, individual firms differ significantly. For example, a small commercial bank has more in common with a savings bank, in terms of the functions it performs, than it does with a large commercial bank. A large commercial bank, on the other hand, performs many of the same functions as an investment banking firm.

UNBUNDLING THE FUNCTIONS OF FINANCIAL DEPOSITORIES

Financial depositories perform two primary groups of functions. They manage portfolios of assets and liabilities and perform a number of information processing functions including financial asset and liability origination, servicing, and brokerage. These functions must first be unbundled so that useful performance measures can be developed for each. This allows each function to be assessed on a stand-alone basis, even though most depositories tend to blend several functions when assessing performance for products and services offered.

Combining functions causes serious evaluation problems since frequently personnel involved in the origination of an asset or liability have nothing to do with its servicing. Similarly, the depository's portfolio is the result of an asset/liability committee's (or a group of some other name) decisions regarding interest rate risk, credit risk, liquidity, and pricing products of the depository. This portfolio is not the responsibility of the origination and servicing units within the firm. Therefore, our first task is to carefully define these activities.

PORTFOLIO MANAGEMENT ACTIVITIES: FINANCIAL ASSET AND LIABILITY CREATION AND TRANSFORMATIONS

Asset and liability transformations describe the products of depositories created by converting their liabilities with one set of characteristics into their assets that may have entirely different characteristics. It is through these transformations that financial institutions simultaneously create desirable financial assets issued by borrowers and others purchased by savers. These transformations account for most of the loan and security (e.g., auto loans, bonds, and business loans) and liability products (e.g., savings accounts, transaction accounts, and certificates of deposits) of depositories.

Traditionally, financial experts emphasized denomination, maturity (or duration), and marketability transformations. In addition to these, intermediaries transform the credit-risk characteristics, the monetary unit or currency, and the extent to which the product serves as a medium of exchange. Consider each of these transformations separately.[1]

DENOMINATION TRANSFORMATION

Denomination transformations involve selling liabilities in denominations that are different from the denominations of the assets they hold. These are the most common transformations performed by intermediaries. Rarely does a saver have the exact amount of funds needed by a borrower. The simplest case is the mutual fund that sells shares in denominations of several dollars, but invests in securities worth thousands of dollars. Other examples include:

• converting various-sized deposits into loans

- creating asset-backed bonds

MATURITY OR DURATION TRANSFORMATION

Maturity transformation relates to the actions of some intermediaries to issue liabilities that have different maturities from the assets in which they invest. For example, most of the liabilities, such as demand deposits and savings accounts, of thrift institutions remain very short-term in nature, while the primary asset of the thrift is a long-term home mortgage. These maturities undergo transformation through the activities of the intermediary. Other examples include:

- issuing long-term asset-backed bonds and investing in short-term loans
- issuing long-term bonds and investing in credit card receivables

MARKETABILITY TRANSFORMATION

Marketability transformations refer to the activities of many financial institutions that hold unmarketable assets and issue marketable liabilities. Their ability to create marketable liabilities while holding unmarketable assets stems, in part, from the economies of scale in their own liquid-asset management activities. Many financial institutions are experts in generating and managing cash that allows them to offer customers such products as transaction accounts. One such advantage is the ability some depositories have to borrow from the Federal Reserve's discount window, the Federal Home Loan Banks, or the Credit Union Liquidity Fund. These federal government credit facilities provide emergency and longer-term borrowing facilities for depositories, allowing depository institutions to hold smaller liquid-asset holdings than otherwise. Other examples include:

- issuing marketable asset-backed bonds using less marketable installment loans
- making a market in swap contracts

CREDIT RISK TRANSFORMATION

Credit risk transformations relate to the differences between the credit risk of an intermediary's assets and that of its liabilities. A large percentage of the assets of most financial depository institutions is below investment grade. Nevertheless, these intermediaries sell liabilities that have investment-grade ratings or the full faith and credit of the U.S. government, thanks to deposit insurance. This is a major transformation. Less well known are the securitization activities of intermediaries. These are financial claims in which intermediaries use overcollateralization to transform the credit quality of a collateralized security. Other examples include:

- issuing senior-subordinated securities using high-risk financial claims
- issuing third-party guarantees on risky debt

CURRENCY TRANSFORMATION

Currency transformations relate to alterations in the currency of financial claims. With the growth in international transactions, the need for currency transformations has grown rapidly. Much of this involves foreign exchange. Somewhat less well known has been the growth in the currency swap market. Commercial banks have been leaders in arranging for foreign institutions to swap funds in two different currencies for repayment at a later date. Examples include:

- selling securities issued in foreign currencies
- creating a mutual fund that holds foreign securities

PROVIDING A MEDIUM OF EXCHANGE

Creating mediums of exchange relates to the payment system products of intermediaries. This is a very specific type of marketability transformation. However, it is traditionally defined separately from that transformation. There has been significant innovation in the creation of new mediums of exchange over the last several decades. The bank credit card is the preferred medium of exchange for many consumers. Other examples include:

- providing electronic payment services
- creating debit cards and preauthorized payment services

CONSTRUCTING THE DEPOSITORY'S PORTFOLIO

Asset/liability managers are responsible for developing and implementing a portfolio strategy for the depository. The performance of the portfolio, however, is not the responsibility of the personnel lending to businesses, the mortgage origination group, or those servicing the credit card portfolio, for example. Rather, it is the responsibility of that senior management involved in asset/liability management described below. Therefore, the depository's portfolio performance should be considered separate from the firm's information processing activities.

PORTFOLIO RISK MANAGEMENT

Portfolio risk management is the heart of intermediation. This function refers to the selection of assets and liabilities the firm chooses to purchase or issue. All risk aspects of the portfolio are considered. The intermediary performs its asset and liability transformation services through portfolio risk management.

By combining the information on customer needs gathered in the brokerage function with information on the status of the firm's portfolio, claims are transformed.

It is important to note that not all financial institutions perform portfolio risk management. Only the subset of financial institutions called intermediaries perform this function. Many financial institutions perform origination, servicing, and brokerage, or some combination of them, with a portfolio of assets and liabilities. Because origination, servicing and brokerage functions can be separated from the portfolio, it is vital to develop performance measures for the portfolio that are separate from this portfolio management function.

It is possible today to develop a portfolio of assets that involves no in-house origination and servicing capability. Through today's well-developed secondary market, mortgages, business loan syndications, and other loans can be purchased without the institution possessing any in-house origination capabilities. Likewise, the firm need not have servicing capabilities since the servicing can be performed by others. The institution relying on the secondary market for some or all of its assets needs to possess only the capability to audit the servicing reports of the servicing firm.

Portfolio risk management uses information from the brokerage and servicing functions to establish the firm's asset and liability strategies. Major activities of the portfolio risk management function are:

- Setting prices for assets and liabilities: performing financial claim valuation analyses in order to determine prices to buy and sell financial claims.
- Managing credit risk: assessing credit risks for purposes of developing an optimal combination of risk and return in an investment portfolio.
- Managing interest rate risk: measuring and managing the risk that the value of a firm's assets rise or fall in value more than the firm's liabilities creating a decline in equity.
- Managing liquidity: managing cash flow.
- Performing arbitrage: engaging in financial claim trading with the purpose of buying in one market and selling in another at a profit or identifying over- and undervalued securities.
- Providing financial guarantees: using the firm's financial strength to reduce the risk of financial claims issued by another party.

Portfolio risk management in many respects calls many of the shots for the other functions within the firm. It is responsible for pricing the assets and liabilities to ensure that the institution can operate profitably. It also has the primary responsibility for interest rate risk management. Analyses that provide quantitative measurements of the interest rate position of the firm submit their reports to the portfolio risk management function.

Although assisted by many other groups within the firm, the portfolio risk management group is responsible for understanding the credit risks inherent in the firm's asset portfolio. Again, credit risk is a portfolio concern since the risks of various types of assets differ, and many respond differently to changing general and local economic trends. Diversification reduces credit risks to manageable levels. Portfolio credit risks must also include any financial guarantees that the firm provides on securities or assets it sells or on securities it guarantees for others. For insurance companies and pension funds, the portfolio risk management group is responsible for managing the mortality risk of the firm or portfolio.

INFORMATION-PROCESSING FUNCTIONS OF INTERMEDIARIES

In order to engage in the transformations just discussed and create the many products and services that intermediaries provide, they must perform certain basic functions. These information-processing functions common to all intermediaries include the following:

1. Financial claim origination
2. Financial claim servicing
3. Financial claim brokerage

Consider each of the functions separately.

FINANCIAL CLAIM ORIGINATION

From an intermediary's perspective, the creation of a financial claim may be an asset or a liability. Origination, called underwriting in the security business, involves the primary activities associated with the creation of a new financial claim–underwriting, document preparation, creation of covenants, as well as the processing activities related to closing the transaction. The relationship between the originating institution and the issuer and owner of a financial claim is shown in Exhibit 3.1. It shows that the originating institution can originate a financial claim for its own portfolio or as an agent for another third-party portfolio.

Origination also involves the selection of the most cost-effective channel of distribution for attracting loan, investment, or liability customers. For a retail bank, for example, deposit gathering might include using branch banks, telemarketing, direct mail, and an agent. Similar choices would be available for the selection of a channel of distribution for a credit card. Originating a financial claim often includes the following activities:

- Credit underwriting (or credit scoring): performing credit analysis to determine the riskiness of a financial claim.
- Financial claim documentation: creating legally binding documents that protect the interests of both the issuer of the claim and its purchaser.
- Development of covenants: creating provisions to reduce the risks of the purchaser of a debt financial claim.

- Collateral review: inspecting and appraising any collateral used to reduce the risk of a debt financial claim.
- Loan disbursement: developing a process to ensure that settlement of a financial transaction protects the parties to it.
- Document control: developing, reviewing, and safeguarding legal documents evidencing rights of the financial claim issuer and purchaser, such as legal documents evidencing ownership of collateral.
- Selection of channel of distribution: selecting the most cost-efficient method of reaching customers for issuing or buying financial claims.

FINANCIAL CLAIM SERVICING

Servicing is a term that often means the collection and payment of principal and interest on assets and liabilities. Actually, however, this function includes everything related to facilitating and monitoring financial transactions. This includes managing the mechanisms, such as demand deposits and credit cards, for operating the nation's payment system. It is also a loan-monitoring function that ensures borrowers are able to adhere to the loan covenants. Another important servicing function relates to collateral control and problem-loan activities. The relationship of the servicing function to the customer issuing a financial claim or owning one and a servicing organization is shown in Exhibit 3.2.

An outsider looking at a financial institution may not think of its servicing responsibilities. If they do understand servicing, then it is likely they will underestimate its importance to the intermediary. In many institutions, most of their human resources are devoted to servicing assets and liabilities.

Financial claim servicing relies heavily on the use of information-processing technology. Computers process the collection of payments on consumer and business loans and update records on the many deposit accounts, mutual fund shares, and insurance policies.

Other servicing activities include loan restructuring, repossessions and foreclosures, collateral disposition, and implementing legal remedies. Loan-servicing units within a financial intermediary must keep good records on the performance of borrowers meeting their obligations under loan contracts. This information permits the firm to respond quickly to default situations. It can also determine how to obtain the best value for repossessed and foreclosed assets.

Exhibit 3.1
Origination Function

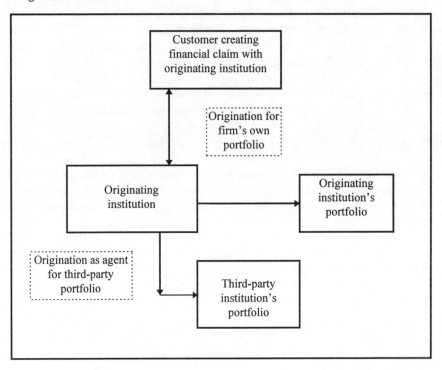

Key servicing activities are

- Processing payments: collecting and processing payments required under the provisions of financial claims such as principal and interest payments.
- Collecting past-due payments: creating a system for collection of past-due payments called for under the provisions of a financial claim contract.
- Controlling collateral: inspecting, inventorying, and appraising collateral over the life of a debt financial claim.
- Safekeeping collateral: providing for the safekeeping of collateral called for under a debt financial claim.
- Monitoring covenants and borrower's financial condition: providing the delegating monitoring services over the life of a financial debt claim.
- Developing delinquency and credit risk reports: providing reports and analyses to assess ongoing credit loss experience to assist in pricing loans.
- Implementing problem loan legal remedies: managing the legal issue related to collection of defaulted debt financial claims.
- Disposing of problem loan collateral: developing systems and procedures for disposing the foreclosed and repossessed collateral.

Exhibit 3.2
Servicing Functions

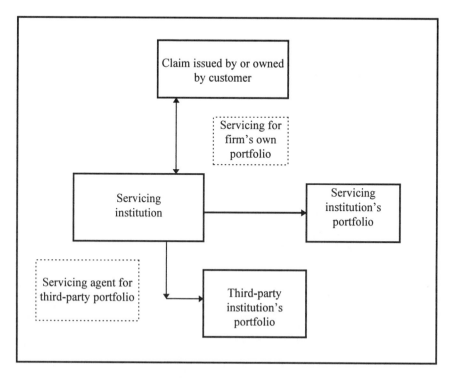

FINANCIAL CLAIM BROKERAGE

Brokerage involves two very significant information-processing functions. It includes identifying potential buyers and sellers of various financial claims the intermediary is interested in, and gathering information related to establishing the market value of a particular claim. The demand for brokerage services derives from the need of financial asset portfolio managers to alter their portfolio's structure in response to changing expectations of risk and return, liquidity, and changing conditions. They do this by buying and selling securities and other financial assets using brokerage services. The relationship between the brokering institution and its customers is shown in Exhibit 3.3. It shows that an institution can broker financial claims into and out of its own portfolio and that of third parties or between third parties.

Brokerage is also involved in reviewing various distribution channels to determine the best price for an asset or liability that might be created by the intermediary. For example, should the firm fund its needs with retail or wholesale funds? Should the firm originate home mortgages or purchase them in the secondary market? These questions are answered through a process involving nothing more than surveying competitor prices for a given financial

Exhibit 3.3
Brokerage Function

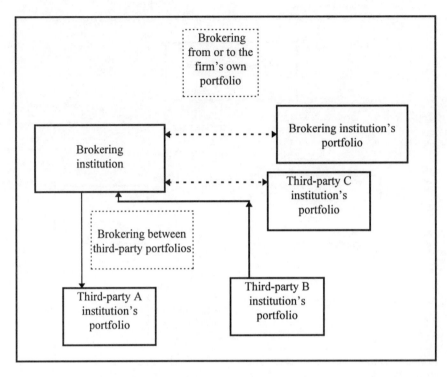

claim, such as a loan or deposit. Key activities of the brokerage function include:

- Acting as an agent for buyers and sellers of financial claims.
- Identifying borrower needs: assessing and developing loan and security products that are desirable to borrowers.
- Identifying saver needs: assessing and developing investment products that are desirable to savers.
- Monitoring prices of financial claims: assessing and evaluating prices of financial claims.
- Monitoring other terms and conditions of the claims: assessing and evaluating risk factors that impact the value of financial claims.

DO IT YOURSELF OR GET IT WHOLESALE?

The need to evaluate the performance of each function performed is especially important in this era of specialization in which most origination and servicing functions can be purchased on a wholesale basis from other institutions. This means that to succeed, each function performed within the firm must be competitive with those available from outside vendors. These competitors are typically highly specialized firms whose success depends on their ability to perform a single function extremely well.

For example, mortgage brokers specialize in mortgage origination at the local level. Mortgage servicers provide specialized mortgage servicing on a regional or national basis. Credit card behemoths have become so successful that some, like FirstUSA, have broken off from a parent organization to become a separate private firm listed on the New York Stock Exchange. A number of specialized high-risk consumer lenders, like the Money Store, have carved out large successful niches in highly specialized markets.

With so many specialized firms providing origination, brokerage, and servicing functions on a wholesale basis, it is more possible than ever before to replace a firm's inhouse functional origination and servicing units with purchased services. Secondary markets in home and commercial mortgages, consumer loans, and business loans are extremely large today. Depositories facing inadequate demand for loans can easily go into the secondary market and buy nearly unlimited quantities of financial assets. These firms can also subcontract out the servicing activities.

THE FINANCIAL CLAIM/FUNCTION MATRIX

The financial claim/function matrix puts each of the four financial functions discussed above into a comprehensive framework. This structure is used to describe the functions performed by depositories on both the asset and liability sides of the balance sheet. The matrix is shown in Table 3.1.

The financial depository is viewed as an information-processing firm that processes and analyzes information in its origination, servicing, and brokerage functions, and manages a portfolio of assets and liabilities. The portfolio management activities are the risk management activities of the firm. Interest rate and credit risks are present whenever the firm takes a financial claim onto its balance sheet. This may be for a very short time, as would be the case of a commercial bank or investment company with a security-trading activity.

The matrix is useful for any depository and is used for the following purposes:

1. To describe the current business activities and markets served by an institution
2. To plan for future new activities and markets
3. To structure a performance evaluation system
4. To assist in organization planning and control
5. To aid in organization control, such as by outlining responsibilities and procedures needed for regulatory compliance

Table 3.1
Financial Claim/Function
Matrix for Assets

	Origination	*Servicing*	*Brokerage*	*Portfolio Management*
Type of Claim				
Government:				
United States				
Agency				
State and municipal				
Business:				
Corporate bonds				
Equities				
Income-property mortgages				
Leases				
Loans				
Household:				
Installment				
Credit card				
Residential mortgages				
Foreign:				
Government				
Business				

The matrix serves as a useful device for describing the financial functions performed and markets served by a financial institution today and those the institution plans to serve in the future. It is also used to structure a performance evaluation system by identifying costs and revenues associated with each function. The matrix is used to identify the activities that must be considered before a financial firm enters a new asset or liability market. As such, it is very useful in strategic and operational planning. If the firm is going to begin offering loans for boat purchases, for example, it must consider what resources are needed for originating and servicing the loans, as well as assessing the impact on the firm's portfolio. Finally, the matrix serves to help identify appropriate organizational responsibilities as the need for controls and a financial firm grows and becomes more complex. Table 3.2 provides a similar comprehensive schematic for the liability side of the intermediary's balance sheet.

One can take every depository and describe it by identifying which functions the firm has chosen and for which financial claim. The difference between firms is determined by management preferences, law, and regulation. The financial claim/function matrix is useful as a structure of any intermediary, from the most complex money center bank to the simplest mutual fund. It makes the focus of individual institutional differences less important, especially in light of the frequent changes in asset and liability powers of institutions.

The structure permits management of financial intermediaries to plan for all necessary functions before becoming involved in new financial claim markets.

WHAT YOU NEED TO DEVELOP THE MATRIX

Developing the financial claim/function matrix is quite simple. All you need to know is the firm's detailed balance sheet, flow of funds account, and organization chart. The first two reports tell you which financial claims the firm deals with. Since each asset and liability has to be originated and serviced by some firm, these statements identify these financial claims. The organization chart specifies which operating units within the firm perform the origination and servicing functions for each asset, liability, and off-balance sheet product and service.

HOW REFINED SHOULD THE ASSET/LIABILITY BREAKDOWN BE?

One of the most difficult problems in developing the matrix is determining the degree of refinement for the assets and liabilities of the firm. A depository might have a consumer credit department that offers ten different types of loan programs. Should each program be accounted for separately? The answer is that the breakdown depends on the organization structure of the firm, the relative size of the programs, and extent to which the two or more products share a common group of personnel or production function.

If the consumer loan program uses the same personnel to originate and service auto loans, second mortgages, unsecured signature loans, and boat loans, then it is reasonable to create a performance report that combines each of these products. Similarly, most institutions have the same personnel responsible for processing all the firm's paper-based checking and NOW account programs. These can safely be combined for purposes of assessing the transaction accounts servicing group's efficiency.

Determining how refined the breakdown should be is a matter of judgment. These decisions usually involve assessing the firm's organization structure to determine the actual work activities of each group of personnel organization structure, as well as whether several products share data processing systems, equipment, and space. Products that share personnel and equipment and space

Table 3.2
Financial Claim/Function
Matrix for Liabilities

	Origination	*Servicing*	*Brokerage*	*Portfolio Management*
Type of Claim				
Transaction accounts:				
Demand deposits				
NOW accounts				
Money market demand accounts				
Time and savings deposits:				
Passbook accounts				
Certificates of deposit				
Capital market financing sources:				
Collateralized debt:				
FHLB advances				
Secured bank loan				
Reverse repos				
Asset-backed securities				
Unsecured debt:				
Negotiable CDs				
Banker's acceptances				
Commercial paper				
Unsecured bank loans				
Debentures				

can usually be combined for purposes of developing the matrix and performance reports.

AN EXAMPLE MATRIX OF THE SMALL COMMERCIAL BANK

The financial claim/function matrix can be used to describe the functions of any intermediary. Consider the case of the hypothetical 1st National Bank of Williamport, South Carolina. This bank of $40 million in assets is located in a small, isolated town. It has few investment options. The balance sheet is shown in Table 3.3. Exhibit 3.4 provides an abbreviated organization chart for the bank

Table 3.3
1st National Bank of Williamsport, South Carolina
Balance Sheet for December 31, 1996

Assets		*Liabilities*	
Cash and U.S. Government bonds	$1,200,000	Demand deposits	$14,000,000
Commercial loans	14,800,000	CDs	22,000,000
Mortgages	11,000,000		
Auto loans	2,000,000		
Building and equipment	1,000,000	Net worth	4,000,000
Total	$40,000,000	Total	$40,000,000

Exhibit 3.1 indicates that the bank has three asset origination units (home mortgages, consumer loans, and commercial loans) and servicing units for each. The bank also holds government securities but does not have to originate or service them. Table 3.4 shows the resulting financial claim/financial function matrix for 1st National Bank. The matrix indicates that the bank originates and services commercial business loans, mortgages, and auto loans and functions as a portfolio manager for these assets. It also purchases government securities where it is a portfolio manager.

On the liability side of the balance sheet, the bank originates demand deposits and certificates of deposit, both of which it services. It acts as a broker for all financial assets and liabilities it originates for its own portfolio.

TYPICAL PRODUCT-LINE FUNCTIONS OF DEPOSITORIES

As depositories get larger, the number of different financial assets, liabilities, and off-balance sheet activities grows significantly. The largest fifty banks may offer hundreds of different products and services for which they might want to develop performance measures. Smaller institutions might choose only five or ten. Some of the most common origination and servicing functions are shown in Table 3.5. Most of the larger brokerage functions are found in the larger depositories operating as security trading departments or as security brokerage subsidiaries of holding companies.

Exhibit 3.4
Organization Chart for 1st National Bank

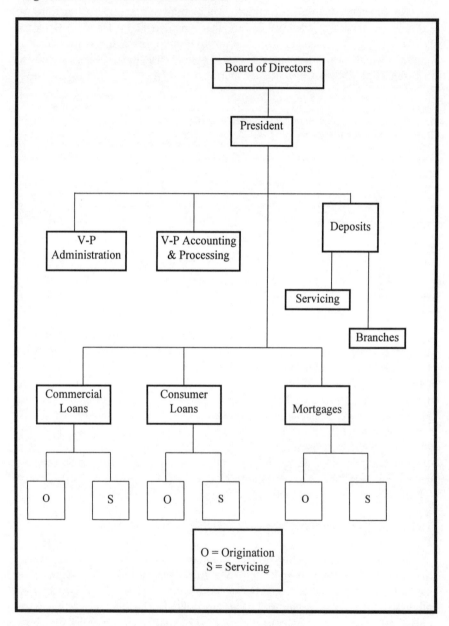

Table 3.4
Financial Claim/Function Matrix for Assets and Liabilities
1st National Bank of Porter, Indiana

	Origination	*Servicing*	*Brokerage*	*Portfolio Management*
Assets:				
Government:				
United States				X
Agency				
State and municipal				
Business:				
Corporate securities				
Mortgages				
Leases				
Loans	X	X	X	X
Household:				
Installment	X	X	X	X
Credit card				
Mortgages	X	X	X	X
Liabilities:				
Demand deposits	X	X	X	X
Certificates of deposit	X	X	X	X

Ultimately, each institution must determine the appropriate breakdown of its origination, servicing and brokerage functions by product and service. This breakdown should be consistent with the firm's organization structure to make the performance measure useful.

Table 3.5
Common Origination and Servicing Functions of Depositories

Common Origination Functions by Product or Service:
    Business loans
    Equipment leases
    Home mortgages
    Income-property mortgages
    Construction loans
    Auto loans
    Credit card receivables
    Other consumer loans (RV, boat, signature)
    Household transaction accounts
    Business transaction accounts
    Time and savings deposits
    Currency and interest rate swaps

      Student loans
      Caps and floors
      Forward contracts
Common Servicing Functions by Product or Service:
      All the above origination products
      Security transfer
      Data processing services for others
      Cash management services
      Lock-box services
      Trust services
      Debit services
      Payment processing
Brokerage Functions by Product and Service:
      Government and agency securities
      Mortgage securities
      Derivatives
      Asset-backed bonds
      Currencies
      Stock and bond security
      Insurance

SUMMARY

This chapter provides that basic framework for identifying the functions performed by all financial institutions. The four basic functions of origination, servicing, brokerage and portfolio management permit financial institutions to develop products and services through financial transformations.

The unbundling of financial functions allows management to identify the roles and responsibilities of each operating unit within the firm. This is essential to the development of performance measures.

The financial claim/function matrix introduced here provides a simply handy way to describe even the most diversified and complex financial institutions. The matrix also provides a schematic that is convenient for use in strategic planning.

NOTE

1. Robert C. Merton, Professor at Harvard Business School and Past-President of the American Finance Association, provides a similar classification system of the functions of intermediaries, which includes: (1) a payment system for exchange of goods and services; (2) a mechanism for pooling funds to undertake large-scale indivisible enterprise; (3) a way to transfer economic resources across geography and time; (4) a system to manage uncertainty and risk; (5) a system to provide price information; and (6) a system to deal with transactions involving unequal information between the buyer and issuer of securities and incentive problems. See Robert C. Merton,

"A Functional Perspective of Financial Intermediation," *Financial Management,* Summer 1995, pp. 24–41.

Chapter 4 . . . .
The Basics of Product-Line Performance Measurement

INTRODUCTION

A variety of performance measurement systems have been used by depositories for years. All these systems involve distributing the firm's expenses and revenues among the firm's various products and services. Some of these systems treat each type of asset as if it is a profit center and attempt to allocate all the revenues associated with that asset, such as interest and fees, and the costs related to originating and servicing the asset and credit losses. Few of these systems treat the depository's liabilities as a profit center, however, which is a serious weakness.

Another weakness of most of these product-line performance measures is that they often include in their design many costs over which the division has no control. This seriously reduces their validity. Avoiding this problem is done only by breaking down functions of the firm. Without a breakdown of these functions, such as those described in Chapter 3, it is too easy to hold a division accountable for results over which it has no control.

This chapter provides the basics of product-line performance systems. It answers the questions: (1) What should be measured? (2) Which classification systems should be used for organizing revenues and costs? and (3) How should we measure performance?

WHAT SHOULD BE MEASURED?

The primary issue in developing performance measures is deciding what should be measured. To answer this question involves determining the appropriate degree of disaggregation of the firm's revenues and costs. The appropriate level of disaggregation depends on two issues. First, it depends on how large the product-line unit is in terms of revenues and costs. A unit that is too small is best combined with another unit so long as the organizational reporting relationship is the same. Second, the firm must decide whether each unit responsible for originating assets should be held responsible for the investment performance of those assets once they are added to the portfolio.

Concerning issue one, there are many instances when it is not cost-effective to treat every product separately. Many products and services are produced by the same groups of people using the same equipment or data-processing systems. These products can safely be combined together for purposes of performance measurement. Checking accounts and NOW accounts, for example, are similar products which are originated and serviced by the same people and typically serviced using the same equipment and computer systems.

Issue two is more difficult and important to resolve. The functional breakdown described in Chapter 3 makes a the case for holding the producers of assets, liabilities, and other information and data-processing services responsible for the origination, servicing, and brokerage functions, but not the portfolio management function. In most depository firms, the gatekeeper for the portfolio is the firm's asset/liability committee (ALCO), or similar group. It is not the firm's origination and servicing groups that determine which assets and liabilities are included in the portfolio and the rates of interest to be charged borrowers and offered savers. This is not to say that the asset originators have no responsibility for quality credit underwriting. The portfolio manager must determine the overall risk tolerance of the portfolio and the asset originators must meet or exceed the agreed-upon risk guidelines when underwriting loans. However, the originator's responsibilities end when they successfully meet the underwriting guidelines established by the portfolio manager at the time the assets are originated. If an economic downturn causes credit losses to increase, it is not the fault of the origination group so long as they meet the underwriting guidelines on the front end.

This job of establishing underwriting standards is typically done by an ALCO-like group responsible for such global portfolio issues as credit risk diversification, interest rate risk management, liquidity, and pricing. These global issues cannot be addressed by having each product-line group be responsible for only a small portion of the firm's assets and liabilities. How does each group that creates these assets finance them, for example? If the origination and servicing groups don't control the financing of the assets, certainly shouldn't be held responsible for the net interest income that results for owning them.

For these reasons, it is strongly advocated that the firm develop performance measures using the functional breakdown described in Chapter 3. This breakdown separates the firm's asset and liability acquisition activities from the portfolio management function.

WHAT REVENUES AND COSTS ARE RELEVANT?

The next job in developing performance measure systems is determining which revenues and costs are relevant to the performance measure. The traditionally measured direct revenues of depository firms are of three types: (1) interest income; (2) capital gains and losses on assets sold; and (3) explicit fees and brokerage income.

This breakdown does not measure the indirect revenues of the firm. Indirect revenues are those charges that are embedded into the loan interest rate charged to compensate the firm for the costs of origination and servicing the asset. Studies have shown that it costs depositories about 50 to 150 basis points per annum on the unpaid balances to service an auto loan portfolio depending on the credit quality and 12 to 20 basis points to service high-quality home mortgages. These origination and servicing revenues are sometimes charged to the borrower directly, but typically are embedded into the interest income on the loans. This portion of interest income is really a return to the firm for performing the origination and servicing functions.

When a firm originates assets and liabilities, it must earn revenues from various sources sufficient to cover the costs of origination. Usually, however, depositories do not charge explicitly to cover these costs. Some assets, such as mortgage loans and commercial business loans, typically earn explicit origination fees that serve to offset some or all of the costs associated with the origination of the assets. However, servicing costs are typically charged indirectly as a portion of the interest earned on the asset. In recent years, the accounting standards under GAAP have been modified to require firms to amortize the costs and revenues of origination over the expected life of the asset. This accounting convention does not apply to the servicing of the asset, however. The problem of covering the cost of origination and servicing is even more serious in the case of liabilities. Deposit interest rates alone do not reflect the full costs of origination and servicing of these contracts. Therefore, the true costs of these funding sources are much higher than reflected by the interest costs alone.

The fact that some portion of the firm's interest income really represents indirect revenue associated with origination and servicing adds a level of complexity to the development of performance measures for its origination and servicing functions. While the separation of these revenue sources is a difficult job, it is not impossible, as will be shown in Chapter 5.

EXPENSE ALLOCATION APPROACHES

Before discussing product-line measures, it is necessary to explain how expenses are allocated to the various product lines. Two basic approaches are used to allocate expenses to product-line profit centers, the fully allocated and marginal contribution expense approaches.

FULLY ALLOCATED EXPENSE APPROACH

The purpose of the fully allocated expense approach is to ensure that all costs of the firm are allocated to some revenue producing unit or other. The fully allocated process involves identification of all direct costs associated with operating each profit center and allocation of all indirect costs back to each profit center. The indirect costs are based on a process of assessing these costs in relation to the degree of support the indirect cost centers provide the product-line profit centers. An example of a fully-allocated profit center is shown in Table 4.1. Here, the direct and indirect costs of operating a product-line unit are identified. Needlesstosay, the cost allocation process is controversial and subject to considerable disagreement within the firm. No unit wants to be charged indirect costs. This issue is covered in Chapter 10.

Table 4.1
Fully Allocated Profitability Model for Auto Lending Department

> Net revenue
>   Direct expenses:
>   Salaries and benefits
>   Furniture and equipment
>   Heat, light and space
>   Telephone
>   Travel, entertainment, and professional fees
>   Other direct expenses
>   Total direct expenses
>   Indirect expenses:
>   Data processing
>   Legal
>   Human resources and training
>   Senior staff and board of directors
>   Marketing
>   Other indirect costs
>   Total indirect costs
>   Income (loss) before taxes

The advantage of the fully allocated approach is that all the costs of the firm are allocated. This may sound like a trivial accomplishment, but as anyone knows who has performed cost allocations, it is very easy to end up with a group of costs put into an "unallocated" account. These are costs of the firm that none of the profit centers will accept responsibility for. Most profit centers show little interest in picking up part of the costs of the board of directors, external auditors, outside accounting firms, lawyers, or investment bankers. Yet, all these costs must be covered for the firm to make a profit.

The fully allocated approach also has the advantage of creating a healthy (or, if allowed to unhealthy) tension within the firm concerning the value of the services received from the indirect support staff centers such as human resources, accounting, data processing, and legal. This process is healthy if it motivates each indirect cost center to be more responsive to the profit centers it serves. Each staff support group will want to justify the value of the services it provides. The approach also allows management to assess the organization structure of each indirect service provider. Sometimes it turns out that the services of a staff support unit are used almost exclusively by only one profit center. If that's the case, it may be worthwhile to turn the indirect service center over to the profit center for reporting purposes.

Knowing the full costs of each profit center provides a means to assess and compare the efficiency of each profit center to those of competitors and other providers of the service. Some of these outside providers may be willing to provide the service to the firm at lower costs and replace the in-house unit. For example, more depository firms have replaced their data processing in-house staffs with private service providers. Still others use loan brokers to originate assets and outside servicers to service some of the assets held in portfolio, rejecting in-house units.

MARGINAL CONTRIBUTION EXPENSE APPROACH

Another commonly used approach to allocating expenses is to charge the profit center only for those direct expenses related to the organization's activities. This marginal contribution expense approach does not charge the unit for all the indirect (overhead) costs that support the unit. The rationale for using the marginal contribution approach is that it allows management to assess the marginal profit contribution of a unit. This makes some sense if one assumes all the indirect costs would be unaffected if the unit under review were eliminated. Needless to say, the management of all the operating units of the firm cannot simultaneously assume that all indirect expenses are fixed costs that would be unaffected if their unit were eliminated. This approach often leads to the unrealistic result that all the profit centers are profitable while the firm as a whole registers a loss.

Consequently, the use of the marginal contribution approach is justified only under certain restrictive situations, such as when a revenue-producing unit is being evaluated over a short-term time frame. For example, if a unit is a candidate for elimination, or is suffering from a temporary cyclical downturn, then as long as the unit is covering its marginal costs and contributing something to covering indirect costs, the unit's continued operation can be justified. A profit statement for a unit measured on the marginal component expense approach is shown in Table 4.2.

COST ALLOCATIONS FOR STAFF SUPPORT UNITS

One complication in the cost allocation process stems from the fact that staff support units provide services for other staff support units. Consequently, there has to be a process for allocating these staff support expenses so that they are ultimately charged to the product-line profit centers. This is done by first making the staff support cost allocations to the staff support units before they are made to the product-line profit centers. Once this is done, the cost allocations to the product-line profit centers will be inclusive of all the staff support expenses.

Table 4.2
Marginal Contribution Expense Approach for Auto Lending Department

> Net revenue
> Direct expenses:
>   Salaries and benefits
>   Furniture and equipment
>   Heat, light and space
>   Telephone
>   Travel, entertainment, and professional fees
>   Other direct expenses
> Total direct expenses
> Income (loss) before taxes

CLASSIFYING PRODUCT-LINE PERFORMANCE SYSTEMS

Traditional performance measures have classified revenues and costs using a number of alternative systems over the years. Each of these is briefly discussed along with those most consistent with the functional performance system in Chapter 3. Four systems are considered: (1) by organizational division; (2) by location; (3) by customer group; and (4) by product and processing group.

PERFORMANCE ASSESSMENT MODEL CLASSIFIED BY ORGANIZATIONAL DIVISION

One of the most common classifications for a performance management system is by organizational division (e.g., business lending, mortgage lending, auto leasing, etc.). The easiest way to segregate revenues and costs using the organizational division is to treat each organizational unit as if it is a mini-intermediary that manages its own portfolio of assets it originates, services, and finances using the firm's liabilities. This classification system is typically developed using one of the two basic approaches for allocating costs discussed above. The problem with this approach is that it makes the inaccurate assumption that the management of divisions have authority over portfolio management functions, but, in fact, they do not. Consequently, the performance systems presented in this book do not support the use of the organizational division approach.

PERFORMANCE ASSESSMENT MODEL CLASSIFIED BY LOCATION

Depositories have offices located nationwide and internationally to a degree never before anticipated. The greatest numbers of these offices are branches designed primarily to originate deposits and loans and to service existing deposits. Many others are loan origination offices for commercial loans and mortgages. With so many offices, it is common to establish performance measures based on geographical location.

Some financial depositories use performance systems that treat deposit-gathering branches that originate loans as if they are stand-alone intermediaries. For the same reasons discussed in the previous section, the performance models proposed in this book reject this approach since the managers of these branches don't control product pricing, interest rate risk, liquidity, and credit risks that are necessary to control in order to properly manage an investment portfolio. As discussed in Chapters 8 and 9, the model used to evaluate deposit-gathering branch performance assumes the primary purpose of these offices is limited to originating financial asset and liability products and servicing them.

The use of location as a performance assessment classification is limited in this book to deposit-gathering branches and loan origination offices. These are discussed in Chapters 8 and 9.

PERFORMANCE ASSESSMENT MODEL CLASSIFIED BY CUSTOMER GROUP

Customer profitability models have long been used by commercial bankers. Many of these models are found in commercial bank management textbooks, making it unnecessary to provide in-depth discussions of them. These models were especially important years ago when depositories were under deposit rate controls and were forced to compete for customers by offering free or low-priced services to compensate important customers for the low-cost deposit balances they provided. This is still a consideration today, but with the deregulation of pricing, it has become less of an issue. Depositories are increasingly requiring every product and service to stand alone from a profit and loss perspective. As this trend continues, the need for customer profitability models is reduced.

A typical customer profitability model like that shown in Table 4.3, has three revenue and four expense components. The three revenue components include: (1) investment income earned on customer deposits held in the depository; (2) additional interest earned as a result of compensating balance requirements on some business loans; and (3) loan interest and fees earned. The four expense components include: (1) the cost of providing services that are offered free or below cost to customers; (2) the cost of supplying funds, both debt and equity, to make the loans outstanding to the customer; (3) loan servicing costs; and (4) default risk cost. These models become complicated due to the impact of reserve requirements when determining revenues and because of the difficulty in determining the marginal costs of services supplied to important customers.

Customer profitability models can be used independently from all the other models presented in this book.

PERFORMANCE ASSESSMENT MODEL CLASSIFIED BY PRODUCT AND PROCESSING ACTIVITY

Most depositories are functionally organized around products and processes. Employees view themselves as working for the credit card servicing unit, for example, or the commercial lending department. Most employees in a depository can explain the nature of their work and can easily differentiate between origination, servicing, or brokerage activities. The origination and servicing functions employ most people in depositories. Few employees in depositories are involved in portfolio management activities. These activities are reserved for analytical types who run models to manage interest rate risk, financial asset valuation, credit diversification and risk, and cash flow forecasts. Even in the largest depositories this group usually represents only a small percentage of all employees.

Table 4.3
Customer Profitability Model

> Revenue:
>> Investment income on customer deposit balances
>> Fee income
>> Loan interest on outstanding loan balances
> Expenses:
>> Interest on debt and deposits used to fund loan(s)
>> Marginal costs of services supplied to customer
>> Cost of servicing loans and deposits
>> Default risk (average of similar risk assets)
> Revenue less costs
> Customer profit (loss)

Employees who work in branches probably have the hardest time classifying themselves. That is because many do not think of opening a checking account or a CD as an origination activity. Others would have a tough time considering the job of reconciling the ATM machine to be a servicing activity. Yet, this is exactly what these personnel do and, therefore, they are treated as such in the performance models presented in later chapters.

The fact that most employees know the functions they perform makes it fruitful to develop a performance system that is consistent with the firm's organization structure. This has several enormous advantages. A performance system defined by product and process, if properly constructed, produces the following benefits. It will (1) assess only those activities over which the employees are responsible; (2) provide accountability; and (3) easily be adapted for the development of incentive programs.

A performance reporting system organized around product and process includes the components shown in Table 4.4.

SPECIAL PROBLEMS WITH ALLOCATING SPACE COSTS

The models used in this book recommend fully allocating the costs of the firm, both direct and indirect, to the product-line profit centers. For most costs, this is a rather straightforward process. One major exception to that is space costs. Most larger depositories occupy a mixture of owned, rented, or leased space. Making matters difficult is the fact that space decisions usually are made over a period of many years. This makes such cost line items as rent, depreciation, property taxes, heat and light, and other costs directly related to space a function not only of the intrinsic, or market, value of the space to the group occupying it, but also a function of when and what type of space occupancy contract was put in place.

Table 4.4
Product and Process Profitability Performance Statement

Origination, servicing, or brokerage income
Direct costs:
    Salaries and benefits
    Furniture and equipment
    Heat, light and space
    Telephone
    Travel, entertainment, and professional fees
    Other direct expenses
Total direct expenses
 Indirect expenses:
    Data processing
    Legal
    Human resources and training
    Senior staff and board of directors
    Marketing
    Other indirect costs
Total indirect costs
Income (loss) before taxes

This is an especially important problem for branch offices. Typically for large- and medium-sized firms the branches occupied include both owned property purchased possibly years ago whose improvements are virtually fully depreciated and other properties that may have been leased at current market rates within the last year or so. When comparing the costs of operating these two offices, usually the older one that has the benefit of using the owned property will have a huge cost advantage. In actuality, however, the unit occupying the owned branch should bear an additional opportunity cost. This is the opportunity rent that could be charged to a third-party firm that might be interested in using some or all of the space if the firm owning it chose to lease or sell it.

In the case of these offices, it is necessary to make an adjustment in the occupancy costs of offices to reflect the true market value of occupancy. Many firms with owned facilities will find that their occupancy costs for product-line profitability reporting purposes will be higher than the lower GAAP-accounting cost basis. Other branches that may have been overimproved, and could not be rented to a third party at a rental rate that would cover the firm's accounting occupancy costs, might actually experience a decline in occupancy costs from that shown on the GAAP-produced accounts.

The result of these adjustments is a set of unallocated costs and revenues assigned to a dummy account. This dummy account can then be allocated to each product-line profit center using some formula such as total square footage used or number of employees in each center.

SELECTING THE RIGHT MODEL TO SUIT YOUR PURPOSE

The selection of the most appropriate expense allocation model is dependent on the firm's objectives. In Chapters 7, 8, and 9, three performance evaluation models are presented. The first is a product-line performance model used to assess performance of origination, servicing, and brokerage units within the firm. For purposes of these systems, the product and process performance classification approach is selected. The second and third performance systems are for branches and loan origination offices. For these systems the geographical assessment model is utilized.

In the case of all these systems, a fully allocated expense model is utilized. Experience has shown that operating units can usually demonstrate that they are profitable if the indirect costs of the firm are ignored. This frequently occurs when the marginal cost model is used and can result in the conclusion that the operating units are profitable while the firm as a whole loses money. The other problem with the marginal cost model is that it creates staff support units that feel they are unaccountable for the services and costs they incur that are charged to the operating units. A good performance system should encourage staff support units to act accountable to the profit centers they serve.

SUMMARY

At the heart of the development of any performance measure is the proper classification of each product-line profit center's revenues and costs. This is a difficult problem for depositories since under GAAP accounting most of the revenues associated with servicing and origination activities are included in the interest income earned on the assets or ignored in the case of deposit liabilities.

The other problem is that profit centers typically don't want to bear the costs of overhead expenses. However, for a firm to be profitable, the profit centers must ultimately cover all the costs of the firm. The selection of the fully allocated expense model is based on this rationale.

Finally, the performance models designed use classification by type of processing activity, product and office location.

Chapter 5 . . . .

Traditional Measures of Depository Performance: Strengths and Weaknesses

INTRODUCTION

Financial ratios are the traditional measures of performance used by management and directors, current and prospective shareholders, creditors, and regulators to assess financial strength and operating performance of financial firms. These traditional measures have strengths and weaknesses. Their strength is that they provide a method to assess the firm's performance on an aggregate basis. On the other hand, they provide little insight into the performance of managers narrowly involved in origination, servicing, and brokerage activities.

Since performance analyses usually involve the important and familiar areas of operations, this chapter overviews the general measurement tools—financial ratios, that is—applicable to all financial depository firms.

TYPES OF RATIO COMPARISONS

As with nonfinancial firms, there are several types of ratio comparisons that financial analysts, owners, managers, and regulators use to analyze performance, specifically the time-series analysis, cross-sectional analysis, and a combined analysis shown in common-size statements. Here's a quick review.

TIME-SERIES ANALYSIS

Time-series analysis looks at the financial performance of a firm over time. By comparing present to past performance through ratio analysis, we can detect improving or deteriorating performance. However, decision makers must identify whether any change over time follows the business cycle, signals an important emerging trend, flags a serious managerial or operational flaw, or simply confirms the firm's expected outcome of its business strategy. The key point to remember is that any change—or the lack of change when change was planned—merits further investigation in order to project future performance and plan necessary courses of action.

Table 5.1 depicts a hypothetical time series analysis of the return on equity (ROE) of State Federal. Table 5.1 shows that the ROE of State Federal has been volatile and trending down over the period covered by the analysis.

CROSS-SECTIONAL ANALYSIS

Cross-sectional analysis compares the financial performance of one financial institution with that of others at a given point in time. This analysis of financial ratios enables decision makers to compare different branch operations of a single firm, different competitors within a certain market, or different types of firms within the financial services industry. Studying differences in performance against the market leader often enables financial managers to identify major operational differences, thereby getting new ideas for ultimately improving the underperformer's efficiency. Analyzing deviations in performance from the industry norm gets managers closer to potential problems as well as opportunities. This form of ratio comparison provides a snapshot of the institution's financial ratios in comparison to a peer group, or one or more competitors. Table 5.2 provides a cross-sectional financial ratio financial ratio analysis of a hypothetical commercial bank and several of its competitors.

In Table 5.2 apparently the First Bank does not compare well on a financial performance basis with its primary competitors. The bank's profitability as measured by return on equity is below the competition's, its capital position measured by net worth to total assets is lower than the competition's, and its expenses are higher for the period shown in the analysis.

COMBINED ANALYSIS

A particularly effective approach to ratio analysis is to combine time-series and cross-sectional analyses in a combined analysis. The combined analysis makes it possible to compare financial rations overtime and with competitors or per groups. Table 5.3 shows the return on equity for First Bank and its peer group over a period of time. The table shows that First Bank has experienced lower and more volatile returns on equity than its peer group for the period shown in the analysis.

Table 5.1
Time-Series Analysis Percent Return on Beginning-of-the-Year Equity for First Bank: Quarterly 1995–1996

Institution	1995				1996			
	I	II	III	IV	I	II	III	IV
First Bank	-0.2	12.2	9.0	8.0	12.4	5.6	8.0	6.5

Table 5.2
Cross-Sectional Financial Ratio Analysis of First Bank and Two Competitors (dollars in millions)

Financial Ratio	Institution Name		
	First Bank	Second National Bank	Country Bank
Net worth to total assets	6.70%	7.30%	8.10%
Return on equity	8.50	11.20	12.50
Operating expenses to total average assets	4.02	3.40	3.24

Table 5.3
Time-Series Analysis Percent Return on Beginning-of-the-Year Equity for First Bank and Peer Group: Quarterly 1995–1996

Institution	1995				1996			
	I	II	III	IV	I	II	III	IV
First Bank	-0.2	12.2	9.0	8.0	12.4	5.6	8.0	6.5
Peer Group	12.3	14.5	10.9	11.8	14.5	8.7	10.0	12.3

COMMON-SIZE STATEMENTS

Common-size statements combine the results of time-series analysis and cross-sectional analysis. The common-size statement depicts percentages of total assets using data from the balance sheet and total revenue using data from the income statement. Analysts typically use these statements to contrast a firm's financial results over time or with its market group, to identify trends in the industry or to pinpoint specific shortcomings or strengths of the firm compared to the norm. Common-size financial statements also help to simplify comparisons between institutions with difference in asset size. Tables 5.4a and

Product-Line Performance Evaluation Systems

5.4b provide examples of common-size income statement and balance sheet for
a hypothetical commercial bank.[1]

Table 5.4a
First Bank Common-Size Income Statement and Supplemental Data
(dollars in millions)

Item	1996 Actual revenue	% of total	1995 Actual revenue	% of total	1994 Actual revenue	% of total
Total income	$410	100%	$380	100%	$337	100%
Interest income	375	91.5	350	92.1	310	92.0
Interest expense	280	68.3	260	68.4	220	65.3
Net interest	95	23.2	90	23.7	90	26.7
Net interest margin	35	8.5	30	7.9	27	8.0
Noninterest income	87	21.2	80	21.1	72	21.4
Noninterest expense	87	21.2	80	21.1	72	21.4
Provision for credit losses	12	2.9	10	2.6	10	3.0
Net operating income before tax	31	7.6	30	7.9	35	10.4
Taxes	9	2.2	8	2.1	9	2.7
Net income after taxes	22	5.4	22	5.8	24	7.1
Shares outstanding (000s)	2,000		1,900		1,900	
Earnings per share	11.00		11.58		12.63	
Dividends per share	8.00		7.80		7.80	

Table 5.4b
Common-Size Balance Sheet and Supplemental Data
(dollars in millions)

Item	1996 Actual amount	% of total	1995 Actual amount	% of total	1994 Actual amount	% of total
Assets:						
Cash and due from banks	$182	7.0%	$173	7.2%	$163	7.1%
Investment securities	416	16.0	360	15.0	322	14.0
Federal funds and reverse repos	312	12.0	240	10.0	207	9.0
Loans	1,661	63.9	1,598	66.6	1,580	68.7
Premises and equipment	29	1.1	29	1.2	28	1.2
Total assets	$2,600	100%	$2,400	100%	$2,300	100%
Liabilities:						
Core deposits	$1,872	72.0	$1,680	70.0	$1,564	68.0
Negotiable CDs	78	3.0	96	4.0	138	6.0
Short-term borrowings, fed funds and repos	234	9.0	240	10.0	276	12.0

Long-term debt	104	4.0	96	4.0	69	3.0
Other liabilities	65	2.5	72	3.0	57	2.5
Total liabilities	$2,353		$2,184		$2,104	
Preferred stock	0	0.0	0	0.0	0	0.0
Common stock	247	9.5	216	9.0	196	8.5
Total new worth	247	9.5	216	9.0	196	8.5
Total liabilities and net worth	$2,600	100%	$2,400	100%	$2,300	100%
Book value per share	$123.50		$113.68		$103.16	
Market value per share	$140.00		$155.00		$165.50	

Supplemental Data:
Off-balance sheet commitments	$1,234	$1,129	$1,075
Standby letters of credit and foreign office guarantees	204	197	209
Other letters of credit	20	89	10
Total commitments	$1,458	$1,415	$1,294
Net loan charge-offs	$13.5	$12.9	$11.0

LIMITATIONS OF RATIO AND FINANCIAL ANALYSIS

Judgment and experience are essential prerequisites for performing financial ratio analyses. It is important for the analyst to understand how the business being analyzed operates. There are a number of limitations in the development and use of ratio and financial analysis. A few of the most important include the following:

Financial ratios are not all created equal: A review of the annual reports of financial companies will demonstrate the considerable use of financial ratios. Comparing these ratios with several firms will reveal frustrating differences in the exact way these ratios are computed. These differences, which are sometimes very subtle and hard to detect, can produce significant differences when comparing ratios among firms. For example, return on equity is frequently computed as (1) after-tax net income divided by beginning-of-the-year net worth or (2) after-tax net income divided by average net worth over the period under review. These differences can easily lead to inaccurate analyses when making comparisons between firms.

Users of financial ratios are not created equal: Financial ratios are used by actual and potential shareholders, creditors, and regulators. Each of these groups may evaluate the same ratios differently. This is because they have different perspectives and concerns. Creditors and regulators will normally give high overall ratings to institutions with high capital ratios, high loan quality, and low financial leverage. Shareholders, on the other hand, may view these same qualities as signs that management is not maximizing returns on the firm's capital resources. The perspective of the reviewer should be considered when using financial analyses.

Financial firms are not all created equal: A major limitation of financial ratio comparisons of two or more institutions is the differences in functions and activities performed by the firms. As discussed in Chapter 3, the financial functions performed by financial firms are usually very different from one another. This is even more of a problem today with the lowering of regulatory constraints on the powers and authorities between different types of financial institutions.

These differences in functions performed by financial firms translate into significant differences in revenues and capital and labor inputs. This in turn significantly affects the financial ratios produced. This is true for firms of nearly equal size as well. For example, a firm with large loan servicing activities for loans sold to others will experience higher operating expenses as well as noninterest income, all else held constant, without comparably larger assets than a firm of equal size that does not service loans for others.

Equally difficult for the analyst is the evaluation of large well-diversified financial firms. The largest bank holding companies in the United States have so many different subsidiaries and financial functions they perform that they have units that are comparable to investment banking, thrift institutions, mortgage banking, security brokerage, insurance as well as many foreign operators. Unless it is possible to obtain financial data on each of the major functional units, it is very difficult to assess performance using aggregate data.

Another problem in comparing like institutions relates to the impact of foreign exchange on financial firms with international dealings. The Financial Standards Accounting Board's statement number 52 requires the firms dealing with foreign currency to reflect changes in the value of foreign currency in their financial statements. This foreign exchange accounting adjustment will also make financial ratios comparisons more difficult.[2]

TYPES OF FINANCIAL RATIOS

A thorough performance analysis considers several aspects of a firm, among them a firm's profitability, financial and operating risks, including capital adequacy, funding risk, asset credit quality, interest rate risk position, off-balance sheet risk, operating efficiency, and liquidity.

Profitability ratios measure return. Capital adequacy ratios measure risk in the form of financial leverage (the magnitude of risk introduced through fixed-cost financing such as debt or preferred stock) and can signal potential financial distress. The greater the financial leverage, the greater the financial risks and, consequently, the closer the regulatory scrutiny. Operating risk ratios measure the levels of interest rate risk, credit risk, and operating expenses that the firm carries. Funding risk ratios call attention to an institution's risk in borrowing money that depends on the sensitivity or reliability of each funding source to the firm's financial situation. Off-balance sheet risk ratios measure the degree to which an institution extends its financial commitments, engages in swaps and forward transactions in security and foreign exchange trading, and conducts any other business transactions affecting credit, interest rate, and liquidity risks not shown on the balance sheet. The following section walks you through each group of tools measuring the aforementioned aspects of all financial firms.

MEASURES OF PROFITABILITY

The most common measures of financial institution performance are measures of profitability. These measures are used to evaluate how well the firm's management is investing the firm's total capital and raising funds. Profitability is generally most important to the firm's shareholders. However, profits serve as a cushion against adverse conditions such as losses on loans or losses caused by unexpected changes in interest rates. Consequently, creditors and regulators concerned about failure also look to profits to protect their interests. Profitability measures have one serious drawback. They ignore the firm's risk. Therefore, relying on profit analysis alone will not provide an adequate evaluation of a firm's overall performance.

PROFITABILITY ANALYSIS: MEASURES OF FINANCIAL PERFORMANCE

Profitability, in terms of maximizing owner wealth, is one of the primary objectives of any for-profit firm. Profits depend on three primary structural aspects of financial institutions: financial leverage, net interest margin, and nonportfolio income sources. Regulation also impacts profitability. Therefore, whenever comparing profitability among different types of financial institutions, differences in regulation are taken into account. So, when interpreting profitability ratios, financial decision makers must consider other measures of operation, such as overall portfolio performance, capital adequacy, and the interest rate and credit risks that the institution carries.

The two most telling measures of general financial performance are net income to beginning-year equity, return on equity (ROE), and net income to average assets return on assets (ROA). Virtually all shareholder-owned financial intermediaries use the ROE ratio. Depositories, finance companies, and life insurance companies find the ROA measure particularly meaningful.

Return on Average Assets and Beginning-Year Equity
1996–1995

Return on average assets :
Equation: Net income$_t$ ÷ [(Total assets$_{12/31/96}$ + Total assets$_{12/31/95}$) ÷ 2]
Computation: Table 5.4a & b: 1996: $22 mil.÷ $2,500 mil. = .88%

Return on beginning-of-the-year equity:
Equation: Net income$_{1996}$ ÷ Shareholder's common stock equity$_{12/31/95}$
Computation: Table 5.4a & b: 1996: $22 mil.÷ $216 mil. = 10.2%

	1996	*1995*
Actual return on average assets	88%	.94%
Actual return on beginning-of-the-year equity	10.2%	11.2%

Strengths:
   The measures of return on average assets and return on beginning-of-the-year equity have the advantage that they provide a global measure of the firm's financial performance. They are easy to compute and use for comparisons to other institutions and industry data.
Weaknesses:
   These measures ignore the risks inherent in the firm's operations. The risks ignored include financial leverage risk related to the capital structure of the firm as well as operating risks related to interest rate risk, credit risk, and operating risks. Operating risks relate to the size of operating units that increase fixed costs of operations during periods of demand volatility.

A major source of income for depository firms that is typically reported as a special line item on their income statement is noninterest income. The sources of noninterest income relate to origination, brokerage, and servicing and are the subject of Chapter 6. One measure of how successful a firm is at generating revenue apart from the firm's asset portfolio is the ratio of noninterest income to average assets. In recent years, many financial institutions have put considerable effort into generating higher levels of noninterest income.

Noninterest Income to Average Assets
1996–1995

Equation: Noninterest income$_{1996}$ ÷
     $[($Total assets$_{12/31/96}$ + Total assets$_{12/31/95})$ ÷ 2$]$
Computation: Table 5.3: 1996: \$35 mil. ÷
$[(\$2,600$ mil. + \$2,400$) ÷ 2] = 1.40\%$

	1996	*1995*
Actual noninterest income to average assets	1.40%	1.28%

Strengths:
   This measure provides one of the few measures for comparing the ability of a depository to generate revenue from origination, servicing, and brokerage activities.
Weaknesses:

The measure has two significant limitations. First, it ignores the benefit to the firm of origination activities that provide high-rate assets to the firm's portfolio without reflecting the costs of origination of the assets and liabilities. Unless the origination process produces explicit fees and other income from the origination process, the revenue from origination for the firm's own portfolio is largely ignored.

Second, the measure provides no way to assess whether its efforts to generate income from origination, servicing, and brokerage exceed the costs of performing these activities. This measure focuses only on revenue and ignores costs.

The primary measure of the profitability of the portfolio management function of intermediaries is the net interest margin. The net interest margin measures the difference between the total interest income earned on the institution's earning assets and the interest expense on its interest-costing liabilities. The net interest margin for period t is shown in Equation 5.1.

$$\text{Net interest margin}_t = \text{interest income}_t - \text{interest expense}_t \qquad [5.1]$$

The net interest margin is influenced by a number of factors. These factors are important to understand when comparing the net interest margin of several intermediaries, and when analyzing the trend in the net interest margin for a single institution over time. The primary factor affecting the net interest margin is the quantities of assets and liabilities of a firm. Size impacts the net interest margin significantly. As a result, the net interest margin is not very useful when comparing the portfolio management activities of different-sized institutions or in reviewing trends of a single institution that is growing or shrinking. To overcome this deficiency, the net interest margin is scaled by the total dollar amount of earning assets and interest-costing liabilities. The result is the net interest spread, which is expressed as a percentage interest rate as shown in Equation 5.2.

$$\text{Net interest spread}_t = [\text{interest income}_t/\text{average earning assets}_t] -$$
$$[\text{interest expenses}_t/\text{average interest-paying liabilities}_t] \qquad [5.2]$$

A problem with the net interest spread is that the dollar amount of earning assets and liabilities is rarely equal. Thus, firms with unequal dollar amounts of interest-earning assets and paying liabilities or a high level of nonperforming assets experience quite different net interest spreads. In order to eliminate the distortion caused by unequal dollar amounts of assets and liabilities, the net interest margin is frequently computed by taking the interest income and interest expense and dividing them by the average assets of the firm. This produces the net interest margin to average assets shown in Equation 5.3.

Net interest spread to average assets$_t$ = [interest income$_t$ -

interest expense$_t$]/average assets$_t$ [5.3]

The net interest margin, net interest spread, and net interest spread to average assets for 1996 computed using the data in Tables 5.4 a & b are shown in Table 5.5.

The net interest spread and net interest spread to average assets are impacted by many factors that are influenced by management's selection of a portfolio strategy. Paramount in importance is the willingness of management to take interest rate and credit risk. Also of major importance is the selection of funding sources used by the firm. The relationship between the dollar amount of earning assets versus liabilities is a factor that impacts the net interest margin. It is worthwhile to review in greater depth how these factors influence net interest spread and net interest margin to average assets.

Table 5.5
Net Interest Margin, Net Interest Spread, and
Net Interest Spread to Average Assets
1996
(dollars in millions)

Item	1996
Average interest - earning assets (a)	$2,471
Interest income[3] (b)	375
Interest income to average earning assets % (c)	15.18%
Average interest-bearing liabilities (d)	$2,200
Interest cost (e)	280
Interest cost to average interest-bearing liabilities (f)	12.73%
Net interest margin (g) = (b - e)	$95
Net interest spread (I) = (c - f)	2.45%
Net interest spread to average total assets (h) = (g/$2,500)	3.80%

RECENT PROFITABILITY TRENDS

After experiencing a very low rate of profitability during the 1980s, commercial banks have experienced a dramatic improvement in profits during the 1990s. After beginning the decade on a weak note, bank profits shot up in 1992 and remained at high levels into 1996. The improvement in profits is due to four primary forces. First, the economic recovery which began in 1991 ended a period of substantial loan losses and the need to establish loss reserves. This lower loss reserving level continued into 1996. Second, commercial banks have benefited from a sharp reduction in competition. Nearly two thousand thrift institutions were wiped out or merged out of existence, as were over a thousand commercial banks. Third, commercial banks have benefited from the sharp decline in short-term interest rates that bottomed out in early 1994. This sent the cost of funds plummeting for banks. Finally, banks have benefited from government policies. Federal Reserve reserve requirements on some accounts were lowered and Bank Insurance Fund insurance premiums were lowered in 1995 and eliminated in 1996.

Table 5.6 shows several statistics measuring bank profitability from 1990 to 1995.

Table 5.6
Selected Profit Performance Measures for All Commercial Banks
1990–1995

Year	Adjusted net interest margin	Return on assets	Return on equity
1995	3.79%	1.18%	14.72%
1994	3.86	1.17	14.65
1993	3.98	1.23	15.34
1992	3.99	0.95	12.66
1991	3.70	0.51	7.71
1990	3.57	0.47	7.29

Source: William R. Nelson and Brian K. Reid. "Profits and Balance Sheet Developments at U.S. Commercial Banks in 1995," *Federal Reserve Bulletin,* Board of Governors of the Federal Reserve System, June 1996, p. 495.

MEASURES OF FINANCIAL AND OPERATING RISK

The are two primary classifications of risk in the operations of a financial institution: financial risk and operating risk. Financial risk relates to the use of fixed-obligation funding sources such as deposits, bonds, preferred stock, and other debt in the firm's capital structure. Financial institutions are typically highly financially leveraged compared to industrial and commercial firms. Depositories are particularly subject to excessive financial leverage unless regulators act to constrain these firms by imposing minimum capital requirements. This is because these firms can use government-insured deposits to raise funds. These depositors rarely concern themselves with the degree of financial leverage the firm has.

The other source of risk is operating risk. This concerns the risks related to the types of the assets owned, such as credit and interest rate risks, costs and liquidity of the funding sources used, and the efficiency of the firm's origination, servicing and brokerage activities.

CAPITAL ADEQUACY: MEASURES OF FINANCIAL LEVERAGE

Capital adequacy relates to the firm's overall use of financial leverage. Generally, firms with high financial leverage will experience more volatile earnings behavior. As you might expect, regulated financial firms with high financial leverage may find themselves under sharp regulatory eye, with sanctions on permissible activities and diminished flexibility in implementing business strategies.[4]

The adequacy of a firm's capital depends on many variables. A financial firm might choose to have more capital, everything else held constant, in the following circumstances:

1. It holds a high percentage of risky assets.
2. It maintains a large unmatched interest rate risk position.
3. It uses a high percentage of wholesale funding sources.
4. It holds a high concentration of assets in a few markets.

The net worth to total assets ratio tells us about the firm's overall financial leverage relative to those assets held on the balance sheet. The higher the ratio, the lower the financial risk of the company. The reciprocal of the net worth to total assets ratio is the equity multiplier (EM). The EM measures the degree of financial leverage of a financial firm. The greater a financial firm's debt relative to equity, the higher its EM.

Net Worth to Total Assets and Equity Multiplier
Year-End 1996, 1995, and 1994

Net worth to total assets:
Equation: (Total shareholder's equity
            and preferred stock)$_{12/31/96}$ ÷ Total assets$_{12/31/96}$
Computation: Table 5.4b: 1996: \$247 mil. ÷ \$2,600 mil. = 9.5%
Equity multiplier:
Equation: Total assets$_{12/31/96}$ ÷ (Total shareholder's equity
            and preferred stock)$_{12/31/96}$
Computation: Table 5.4b: 1996: 1÷.095 = 10.53x

	1996	1995	1994
Actual net worth to total assets	9.5%	9.0%	8.5%
Actual equity multiplier	10.53x	10.90x	11.76x

Strengths:
    These measures provide simple aggregate measures of financial leverage. They are easily used to compare to industry norms and peers groups.
Weaknesses:
    These measures are of limited value because they are based on accounting values, not market values. Many depositories have sources of shareholder value not reflected in the firm's net worth accounts, such as a large consumer customer base, available cross-selling, undervalued assets, and especially

valuable business franchises. These values are usually reflected in the market value of the firm's common stock even though they aren't reflected in the accounting values. A firm whose market value of equity per share exceeds the firm's book value per share has the advantage of being able to sell equity at prices significantly above the firm's book value. Conversely, a depository with a book value above its market value would have a difficult time adding to its equity base by selling new stock if it was necessary to do so.

These measures also ignore the overall riskiness of the firm's operations. Interest rate, credit, and operating risks are totally ignored by these measures of financial leverage.

Shareholders are very sensitive to the overall performance and future prospects of a company. What about those sources of capital—a large, venerable loan-servicing unit or, in contrast, a plunging portfolio of securities —that do not appear on the firm's balance sheet but affect performance positively or negatively? The capital adequacy ratio, market value of common stock equity to book value of equity per share, helps to highlight the relationship between the firm's market value of assets and liabilities and the corresponding book value. A sharp plummet in the market value of a firm's common stock caused by a deterioration in asset quality might signal financial distress, whereas the long-term ongoing revenue from a large loan servicing unit would add value beyond its accounting worth to the firm.

ASSET CREDIT QUALITY: MEASURES OF CREDIT RISK

Asset credit quality refers to the credit risks embodied in the institution's asset portfolio. An institution with a high percentage of U.S. Government Treasury and agency securities and other high-quality short-term securities has exposed itself to less credit risk than a firm heavily engaged in construction lending for building shopping centers.

The following credit assets are usually considered risky:

1. Consumer loans, generally excluding single-family first mortgages
2. Commercial and industrial loans (loans to business)
3. Income property mortgages
4. Foreign loans
5. Merger and acquisition, research and development, and construction loans

Another criterion in measuring credit quality is the performance of loans on the books, specifically the loan loss experience and delinquency rates of various loan portfolios. One measure of such credit risk is the net loan charge-offs to average net loans (including leases) ratio, which signals the extent to which the firm has written off losses on loans and leases. Typically, the net loan charge-offs (or credit losses) are divided by average net loans and leases to form a ratio that you can compare reasonably to those of any other financial institution.

Market Value of Common Stock Equity to Book Value Per Share Year-End 1996–1994

Equation: Market value per share$_{12/31/96}$ ÷ Book value per share$_{12/31/96}$
Computation: Table 5.4b: 1996: $123.5 ÷ $140.0 = 113%

	1996	1995	1994
Actual market value of common stock equity to value per share	113%	73.3%	62.3%

Strengths:
    This measure provides a method to correct the problem of using accounting values to measure the equity of the firm.
Weaknesses:
    This measure is highly volatile since it is influenced by forces that affect general stock market levels that may not directly impact on the operation of the depository. It also does not provide any insight as to why shareholders view the firm's equity to be worth more or less than its market value.

Analysis of allowances for credit losses on total loans also provides more information about credit risk. The current-period credit loss provision indicates the extent to which financial firms use profits to establish reserves against anticipated future losses on loans and leases. The loan loss provision is based on an assessment of the quality of the firm's asset portfolios. Each type of asset portfolio is evaluated using statistics on delinquency, repossession, foreclosure, and asset disposition to determine the potential loss that the firm can expect to sustain given the deterioration in the quality of the loans. Managers typically set up such reserves to cover losses that they did not expect to charge off until future periods. These loss provisions are somewhat subjective. As a result, accounting firms and regulatory agencies review them carefully.

Net Loan Charge-offs to Average Net Loans 1996–1995

Equation: Net loan charge-offs$_{1996}$ ÷ (Total loans and leases$_{12/31/96}$ + Total loans and leases$_{12/31/95}$) ÷ 2)
Computation: Table 5.4a & b: 1996: $13.5 mil. ÷ [($2,400 mil. + $2,600 mil.) ÷ 2] = .54%

	1996	1995
Actual net charge-offs to average loans	.54%	.55%

Strengths:
    The major strength of this measure is that it approximates actual loan losses as compared to other measures that rely primarily on estimates of losses.
Weaknesses:
    The primary weakness of this measure is that it measures losses on loans well after establishing the initial loss provision. This means that it can lag actual loan credit performance by a significant period of time. Actual charge-offs could easily lag the provision for charge offs by several years, making it a poor measure of the current credit worthiness of the firm's portfolio.

The customary way to express the relationship of credit loss provisions to total loans (including leases) is by the ratio of loan loss provision to average loans.

Loan Loss Provision to Average Total Loans
Year-end Balances
1996–1995

Equation: Loan loss provision$_{1996}$ ÷ (Total loans and leases$_{12/31/96}$ ÷ Total loans and leases $_{12/31/95}$) ÷ 2]
Computation: Table 5.4a & b: 1996: $12 mil. ÷ [($1,598 mil. + $1,661 mil.) ÷ 2] = 0.74%

	1996	*1995*
Actual loan loss provision to average loans	0.74%	.629%

Strengths:
    The primary strength of this measure is that it attempts to measure losses on a current basis. Management and accountants must attempt to estimate the losses that, while they may not yet have been realized, are expected to be realized on the firm's current portfolio.
Weaknesses:
    The major weakness of this measure is that loan loss provisions are based on anticipated losses that may turn out to be poor forecasts of actual losses. Although less a problem in recent years owing to more stringent accounting and regulatory practices, depositories have been known to underestimate losses or delay reporting them until periods when they had unexpectedly good earnings. The latter objective was to smooth earnings and, thereby, make the firm's earnings appear less volatile and, therefore, less risky.
    The other basic weakness with this measure is that it does not relate loan losses to the overall riskiness of the portfolio. Some institutions invest in assets expected to have relatively high credit losses such as credit cards and other consumer loans. These firms will appear to have high credit losses compared to peers and industry averages. In fact, a firm might have losses that are more than

adequately covered by the interest rate charged on the loans in question. In this case, the institution will appear to be more poorly managed than it really is.

Delinquency ratios also provide timely information about the credit quality of such specific asset categories as mortgage loans, credit cards, and auto loans held by the firm. Credit managers can compare these measures to delinquency ratios of other financial firms as well as industry statistics, not just to rate quality of financial assets, but also to see how effectively the firm's overall loan servicing policies are working.

RECENT ASSET QUALITY TRENDS

Asset quality at our nation's depositories has taken a dramatic turn for the better beginning in 1992 and continuing into 1996. Real estate overbuilding in the commercial sector in the 1980s resulted in failure of hundreds of thrifts and huge losses on real estate loans of commercial banks. This is clear from the ratios for loan-loss expense as a percentage on interest-earning assets and nonperforming loans as a percent of total loans, shown in Table 5.7.

Table 5.7
Asset Quality Trends at Commercial Banks
1990–1994

Year	Loan-loss expense as a percent of interest-earning assets	Nonperforming loans as a percent of total loans
1994	0.32%	1.54%
1993	0.53	2.44
1992	0.88	3.34
1991	1.17	3.76
1990	1.11	2.71

Source: Lynn W. Woosley and James D. Baer. "Commercial Bank Profits in 1994," *Economic Review*, Federal Reserve of Atlanta. May/June 1995. pp. 11–31.

INTEREST RATE RISK POSITION: MEASURES OF INTEREST RATE RISK EXPOSURE

Interest rate risk is today one of the most sophisticated areas of analysis within well-run financial firms. Interest rate risk is the risk that a change in interest rates will cause the market value of a firm's assets to move closer to the market value of the firm's liabilities and thereby reduce the firm's equity. The greater the firm's exposure to such an occurrence, the greater is its interest rate risk.

Periodic GAP is the most common measure reported frequently in a footnote to the financial statements of depository institutions. A hypothetical schedule for the institution shown in Tables 5.4a & b is shown below. There are insufficient data in Tables 5.4a & b to develop this schedule. The creation of this table requires estimates of the timing of the cash flows of the firm's financial assets and liabilities.

Periodic GAP Buckets for Various Periods					
Period t	0-30 Days	31-90 Days	91-365 Days	0-365 Days	Over 365
Earning assets	$.65	$.35	$.15	$1.15	$1.40
Sources of funds	$.64	$.36	$.18	$1.18	$1.44
GAP_t	$0.01	-$0.01	-$0.03	-$.03	$.04
GAP_t to total earning assets$_t$	1.5%	-2.9%	-20.0%	-2.6%	2.9%

Strengths:
The principal advantage of the periodic GAP report is its simplicity and versatility. This report easily understood by managers and directors, has few difficult computational disadvantages.
Weaknesses:
Periodic GAP reports have some important limitations, which stem from the fact that GAP reports are computed at a point in time and they cannot properly account for uncertain cash flows and for the repricing limitations of certain assets and liabilities. The following are some of the limitations of GAP reports.
Repricing or Maturity Bunching
The GAP_t report only shows the relationship of repricing assets and liabilities during the period *t*. It does not show the interest rate position of the firm after period *t* or between two periods. This creates a problem when a firm has a large volume of assets or liabilities repricing or maturing during a period between two GAP periods, $GAP_{t+1,t+2}$. The periodic GAP report will not disclose the bunching of asset or liability maturities or repricings. Although the analyst producing the *GAP* report is probably aware of these bunching problems, this is still a limitation of the methodology.
Estimates of Cash Flows
The GAP report is only as good as the analyst's estimates of asset and liability cash flow. It is very likely that some of the assets and liabilities that reprice have prepayment options embedded in them. This is true with mortgages, for example. This means that the GAP report must rely on estimates of the percentage of mortgage principal that will repay during period *t*.
Another problem concerns assets whose repricing is discretionary. Some assets that may be repriced under the terms of the claim contract are rarely repriced, even during periods of interest rate volatility. Credit card receivables,

for example, can be repriced within a short period of time, but they are rarely repriced in practice, even if market rates change by moderate amounts. Other examples are passbook accounts at commercial banks and thrifts and interest-paying negotiable order of withdrawal accounts. The rates on these accounts are rarely changed. This means the analyst is left with the task of making assumptions about whether these assets are in practice more like adjustable-rate or fixed-rate assets. The analyst must then calculate the GAP statement by incorporating these assumptions.

Rate-indexed Assets and Liabilities

Another limitation of the GAP report relates to the fact that when rate-indexed assets and liabilities reprice, there may be caps or other limitations on the magnitude of the adjustment. This usually occurs when the asset includes an *interest rate cap*. An interest rate cap is a contractual limit on the maximum level of the interest rate on an adjustable interest rate financial claim. These caps are found in many adjustable-rate mortgages, for example. Consequently, a firm with many capped adjustable-rate mortgages will appear from the GAP report to have a low interest rate risk exposure even though the assets facing upward adjustments are constrained by the cap.

Income Statement

Another limitation of the GAP report is that there is no stable mathematical relationship between the firm's GAP and its profitability. While it is possible to say that a firm with a positive periodic GAP should perform better in a rising interest rate environment than in a declining rate environment, it is difficult to determine the extent of the income variation.

Off-Balance Sheet Risks

GAP reports usually do not disclose the interest rate risks related to off-balance sheet claims and commitments. Firms with large off-balance sheet investments in loan servicing contracts, for example, do not reflect the risks of prepayment of these assets. The interest rate risks related to options granted by an institution as loan commitments and forward loan sales are not reflected. These risks are, therefore, incorporated in the overall risk assessment of the institution in other ways.

Another assessment of a firm's interest rate position, market value to the book value of the firm's securities, reveals the relationship between the market value and book value of a financial firm's security investments. This schedule shows whether the firm has a potential gain or loss on its holdings of securities based on their current market value. A large portfolio of securities that have unrealized gains or losses may reflect potential profits or losses not revealed by the firm's profitability measures. These schedules also reflect any impact that sharp increases or decreases in open market interest rates may have had on the firm. For this reason and others, the U.S. accounting profession is now mandated through Statement of Financial Institution Standards SFAS Number 115 that all financial firms report this comparison of market to book value in their financial statements, now normally provided as an optional footnote.[5] That's why Table 5.4b does not include these data.

Mark-to-Market of Investment Securities Portfolio December 31, 1996 (dollars in millions)		
Security	*Book Value*	*Market Value*
U.S. Treasury	$14	$15
Other U.S. government	123	120
State and municipal	210	200
Other bonds, notes, and debentures	56	52
Federal Reserve Bank and other securities	145	144
Total	$548	$531

FUNDING RISKS: MEASURES OF OVERALL LIQUIDITY

Funding risks refer to an institution's risk in maintaining liquidity. A depository can borrow funds from retail sources such as deposits from local branches of commercial banks and thrifts or from wholesale sources such as institutionally sold negotiable certificates of deposit, brokered-insured deposits, and other capital market pools of, say, commercial paper. Studies show that small-denomination retail deposits, also called core deposits, will be less price-flexible and interest-elastic and, therefore, more stable than deposits attracted from wholesale distribution channels. The same is true for insurance policies sold to individuals as opposed to those sold to corporate clients by life insurance companies. In general, retail funding risk will be lower than wholesale risk, and higher if the institution relies more on nonretail deposits.

Two measures of funding risk are comparisons of *core deposit sources to total* funding sources, and brokered deposits and other deposits over $100,000 to total deposits. The balance sheet for 1996 in Table 5.4 b provides the needed data to assemble the statement below, which users might find as a footnote to financial statements of commercial banks.

OFF-BALANCE SHEET RISK MEASURES

Today, many of the risks of financial institutions do not show up on the balance sheet. This is because current reporting requirements do not cover a wide variety of activities in which financial firms engage. That does not mean that managers of financial firms should ignore these activities. On the contrary, institutions may have commitments outstanding that could increase both credit and interest rate exposure.

Core Deposits to Total Funding Sources: 1996 (dollars in millions)	
Core deposits	$1,872
Noncore deposits	78
Short-term borrowings	234
Acceptances outstanding	0
Senior long-term debt	104
Other liabilities	65
Subordinated debt	0
Total	$2,353

Equation: Core deposits$_{12/31/96}$ ÷ Total funding sources$_{12/31//96}$
Computation: Table 5.4b: 1996 $1,872 ÷ $2,353 = 79.6\%$

Actual core deposits to total funding sources (12/31/96)   79.6%

Strengths:
The primary strength of the core deposit ratio is that it provides a means to assess the consumer franchise value of a depository. Wholesale deposit sources do not possess the franchise value that is apparent when cross-selling products and services to retail customers.

The core deposit ratio also provides a means to assess the liquidity risk of the firm's liability base. Generally, retail deposits are significantly less volatile than wholesale deposits because retail customers have 100% insurance of accounts.

Weaknesses:
The core deposit ratio does not give the user a clue as to whether the core deposit base is stable or consists of "hot" interest sensitive funds. Many depositories pursue a high rate strategy to attract even retail deposits. This is hard to detect using the core deposit ratio.

Some of the most common off-balance sheet exposures include loan commitments, involving obligations of lending firms to originate loans on demand of a borrower; standby letters of credit, involving obligations of lending firms to provide a backup source of financing to a firm selling commercial paper; and loans sold with recourse, which involve the sale of a loan to another institution with the provision that the seller will repurchase it if the buyer proves that the asset did not perform as contracted.[6]

One measure of off-balance sheet risk is the ratio, loan commitments and standby letters of credit to total assets. Using data from the statement on on-balance sheet commitments in Table 5.4b, a statement such as the one below is commonly shown as a footnote to financial statements of commercial banks.

Commitments Outstanding
Year-end 1996 and 1995

	1996	1995
Commitments to extend credit	$1,234	$1,129
Standby letters of credit and		
foreign office guarantees	204	197
Other letters of credit	20	89
Loans sold with recourse	0	0
Total	$1,458	$1,415

Equation: (Total commitments$_{12/31/96}$ + standby letters$_{12/31/96}$ + other letters of credit$_{12/31/96}$ + loans sold with recourse$_{12/31/96}$) ÷ Total assets$_{12/31/96}$

Computation: $1,458 ÷ $2,600 = 56.1%

	1996	1995
Actual commitments as percent of total assets	56.1%	59.0%

Strengths:

Tables showing off-balance sheet exposures of depositories help to assess the extent to which the firm is adding financial leverage, interest rate risk, and credit risks that are not evident from the firm's capital leverage ratios. They also give the analyst a basis for ascertaining the types of risks the firm is subject to — liquidity, credit, and interest rate risks.

Weaknesses:

The problem with schedules of off-balance sheet transactions is that they do not provide an estimate of the true extent of the risks faced by the depository. A well-matched swap portfolio eliminates interest rate risk, for example. On the other hand, depending on the credit worthiness of the counterparties to the swaps, the depository might face significant or minimal credit risks. The same considerations relate to the other components of off-balance sheet transactions.

OPERATING EFFICIENCY: MEASURES OF INTERMEDIATION PROCESSING

Since financial institutions can perform a variety of financial functions and deal with different types of financial claims, comparing the operating efficiency of firms is no easy task. Each financial firm operates in different markets with vastly different ratios of retail to wholesale asset and liability strategies. Each varies the functions it performs on each of the financial claims it chooses to originate, service, broker, or invest, and pursues different strategies for originating, servicing, and brokering new claims. While higher interest rate margins may offset the operating cost differences and yield higher profits, one firm may appear to operate less efficiently than its competitors. For example, a commercial bank with a high percentage of assets in a credit card activity will generally experience higher operating expenses as a ratio of average assets compared to a bank with a lower level of assets in credit card receivables. Still, the bank with the higher credit card receivables may well have a much higher interest rate margin and greater overall profitability. Operating expenses and noninterest income, rather than total assets, may reflect the effectiveness of these strategic differences. As a result, the most common measures of operating efficiency signal the need for further investigation of performance efficiency or incompetence.

Operating expenses (noninterest expenses) to average assets is the most frequently used measure of operating efficiency. The resulting ratio tends to be higher for highly diversified firms, such as large commercial banks, than for specialized firms such as thrifts because the diversified firms have more expenses related to origination and servicing for their many more different types of financial assets and liabilities. Also, firms that originate and service assets for others tend to have higher operating expenses to average assets ratios because the cost of servicing is included in the ratio's numerator and the loans serviced are not shown in the firm's average assets.

**Operating (Noninterest) Expenses to Average Assets
1996–1995**

Equation: Noninterest expense$_{1996}$ ÷ [(Total assets$_{12/31/96}$ + Total assets$_{12/31/95}$) ÷ 2]

Computation: Table 5.4b: 1996: $87 mil. ÷ [($2,600 mil. + $2,400 mil.) ÷ 2] = 3.48%

	1996	*1995*
Operating (noninterest) expenses to average assets	3.48%	3.40%

Strengths:
    This global measure is easy to compute and understand. It makes comparisons with peer groups and industry data simple.
Weaknesses:
    The measure of operating efficiency is only meaningful for comparisons to firms with virtually identical operating strategies. Firms with different operating strategies will have decidedly different expense ratios.
    A low expense ratio does not always imply an efficient firm. This is because a very efficient firm that generates considerable revenue and value from origination, servicing, and brokerage may be very efficient, but still suffer from a high expense ratio. This is because expense ratios do not take into consideration off-balance sheet operating activities such as loan servicing or the mix of retail to wholesale activities. Wholesale loan acquisitions are substantially less costly in terms of origination costs than retail origination activities. Yet, the firm using the retail strategy might be much more profitable

since it is able to get much higher yields on the loans it originates as compared to those loans purchased wholesale.

RECENT OPERATING EFFICIENCY TRENDS

Despite the massive consolidation going on in the commercial bank and thrift industries, the primary aggregate measures of operating efficiency have not shown any noticeable trend toward increased efficiency. Table 5.8 provides the ratio of noninterest expense (operating expenses) as a percent of total assets at all commercial banks from 1990 to 1994.

Table 5.8
Noninterest Expense to Total Assets at All Commercial Banks
1990–1994

Year	Noninterest expense as a percent of total assets
1994	3.78%
1993	3.95
1992	3.91
1991	3.73
1990	3.50

Source: Lynn W. Woosley and James D. Baer. "Commercial Bank Profits in 1994," *Economic Review*, Federal Reserve of Atlanta. May/June 1995. pp. 11–31.

Overall, the data reflect no clear trend in overall operating efficiency during this period. Since commercial banks have emphasized building noninterest income and pursuing off-balance sheet transactions, it is likely that this ratio will rise or remain high despite industry efforts to cut costs.

FINDING FINANCIAL DATA

Data used for analyses of financial firms is quite easy to obtain for regulated commercial banks and most thrifts. Typically, a firm's data comes from its published financial reports, such as its annual report, quarterly reports, and 10k filings. A number of private data collection firms publish comparative data for commercial banks and thrifts. These include Sheshunoff and Co. and SNL Securities, L.P. Considerable help for publicly traded companies is available from security analysts.

Data for commercial banks, S&Ls, and SBs are available from regulators at the FDIC, OTS, and the Board of Governors of the Federal Reserve System. Performance measures for peer groups are available in the annual report *Uniform Bank Performance* published by the Federal Financial Institution

Examination Council and in the report *Statistics on Banking* published annually by the FDIC. The FDIC also provides quarterly performance data on commercial banks and thrifts in its *Quarterly Banking Profile*. The Federal Reserve's Board of Governors publishes an annual commercial bank performance article in the *Federal Reserve Bulletin*, usually in the June or July issue.

REVISING FINANCIAL RATIOS FOR MEASURING PORTFOLIO PERFORMANCE

Chapter 3 defined portfolio management as those activities concerning the pricing of assets and liabilities, and managing liquidity, interest rate risk, and credit risks. These global portfolio concerns are performed by a decision-making group that has responsibility for all aspects of it. The problem with GAAP accounting conventions is that they don't allocate some of the portfolio's income to the origination and servicing units that incur expenses in the process of providing the assets and liabilities to the firm's portfolio.

In order to use the performance measures discussed in later chapters, it is necessary to adjust various income categories by use of the internal transfers of revenue from the portfolio's interest income to the firm's various origination and servicing units as shown in Chapter 7. One result of this reallocation of interest income is that it makes comparing this adjusted portfolio interest amount with peer groups and industry ratios impossible. However, this is not a problem since the unadjusted GAAP statements will continue to be available.

SUMMARY

The traditional measures of depository performance provide useful aggregate measures of performance to use to compare to peer groups or to compare over time. Each of these measures suffers from limitations related to the fact that a portion of the interest income earned is really compensation for origination and servicing activities performed. Noninterest expenses are similarly aggregated, making it impossible to assess performance of origination and servicing units.

NOTES

1. One caution in the use of common-size statements is that they may encourage simple comparisons of firms that are really not comparable. A $10 million asset bank should not be compared to a $1 billion asset bank since the functions and activities of banks of these sizes are really very different. They therefore do not make good candidates for comparison. Similar problems occur in financial comparisons using industry aggregate data. Industry aggregates may be dominated by very large firms. Consequently, comparisons of smaller firms are not very useful.

2. Foreign currency transactions are covered by FASB-52. This ruling establishes accounting and reporting standards for translation of foreign currency financial

statements and foreign currency transactions. It is the objective of FASB-52 to preserve the financial results and relationships that are expressed in the foreign currency. This is done by converting the financial statements denominated in a currency different from the reporting currency into the reporting currency using appropriate foreign exchange rates.

3.   Typically whenever industry comparisons are made, the interest income of commercial banks is adjusted for the impact of tax-exempt securities held by the bank. Banks that hold large amounts of tax-exempt bonds have lower before-tax interest income than those with few of these bonds even though their after-tax income may be higher. To compensate for this impact this adjustment is done by using the before-tax equivalent interest rate on the tax-exempt bonds when calculating interest income.

4.   The capital requirements for commercial banks and thrifts has been made nearly uniform. Capital is measured as Tier 1 capital composed of tangible equity, including common stock, retained earnings, and perpetual preferred stock, and supplemental capital is made up of subordinated debt, loan-loss reserves, intermediate-term preferred stock, and some other minor items. Financial depositories subject to these capital requirements must maintain a Tier 1 capital ratio of 4 percent and 8 percent for total capital, respectively, of total risk-weighted assets.

5.   SFAS 115 became effective on January 1, 1994. It provides that firms account for certain investments in debt and equity at their current market value if the management of the firm anticipates that the asset will be sold before maturity. The financial assets so classified are marked to their current market value and any difference between that value and its book value is added or subtracted from the firm's equity as a separate component of the equity account on the balance sheet. These adjustments do not immediately affect current income.

6.   Financial Accounting Standards Board interpretation (FASB 139) has effectively limited the ability of depositories to net the value of off-balance sheet derivative contract under GAAP.

Chapter 6 . . . .

Noninterest Income Sources (Origination, Servicing, and Brokerage Revenue)

INTRODUCTION

The importance, sources, and advantages and disadvantages of noninterest income-generating activities are discussed in this chapter. In Chapter 3, the four basic functions of depositories were described. Each of them, origination, servicing, brokerage, and portfolio management, was shown to be a source of revenue and expense for depositories. However, much of the income from these activities does not represent interest earned or expensed on financial assets. Rather, this income results from nonintermediation functions.

WHY NONINTEREST INCOME IS SO IMPORTANT

A number of forces have compelled financial institutions to seek sources of revenue that are not dependent on intermediation. These sources of revenue are called noninterest income. They do not involve interest income or expenses. The most important sources of noninterest income are fees charged for services rendered by intermediaries. This source of income is also referred to as fee-based income. The long-term downward pressures on intermediation profit margins and rising capital requirements are two principal reasons for the growing interest in noninterest income generating activities.

NET INTEREST MARGINS UNDER PRESSURE

During the last twenty years, the traditional depository intermediaries have experienced significant new competition and have lost valuable regulatory protections. Competitive new powers for thrift institutions and significant competition from nonbank intermediaries have reduced profit margins for portfolio management's lending and deposit-taking functions. Thrifts have had to compete with federally sponsored enterprises in mortgage lending, which has reduced their portfolio management profitability. The result has been unprecedented profit pressures. This has led to consolidation and failures.

This profit pressure is evident in the decline during the 1980s in the net interest margin. Until 1980, depositors earned market interest rates on loans and had their deposit rates held below market levels by interest rate ceilings controlled by the Federal Reserve under Regulation Q. This virtually guaranteed a positive net interest margin.

These regulations had another interesting impact. They caused most depositories to compete for customers using nonrate-competitive product and service features. Rather than charge customers the full cost of providing such services as automated tellers, transaction accounts, and convenient service, depositories charged below-market prices in hopes of attracting below-market rate deposit accounts from customers. These nonprice factors had the impact of increasing operating costs and artificially holding down noninterest income that under normal circumstances would have made these services profitable.

During the 1970s through today, competition from investment bankers opened up the money and capital markets to many traditional depository business customers. Government sponsored enterprises competed for mortgages, student loans, and farm loans. These factors created downward pressure on profit margins.

CAPITAL REQUIREMENTS INCREASE IMPORTANCE OF NONINTEREST INCOME

The failure of so many savings and loans, savings banks, and commercial banks in the 1980s and 1990s resulted in legislative- and regulator-mandated increases in capital requirements at insured depositories and insurance companies. Higher capital requirements increase the weighted cost of capital for some depositories. This increase in capital costs is another important reason why depository institutions and insurance companies have developed operating strategies that do not rely on leveraging capital by acquiring assets.

Most noninterest-earning activities do not involve adding large amounts of assets to the balance sheet of the firm. This means that the financial institution can pursue revenue-raising activities without incurring additional regulatory capital requirements. For the most part, financial depository institution regulators ignore the operating risks associated with large origination, servicing, and brokerage activities when establishing equity reserve requirements.

GROWTH IN NONINTEREST INCOME

In the last several decades, most depositories have stressed the growth of noninterest revenue sources. This pressure to build noninterest income has accelerated in the 1980s and 1990s. Good measures of the growing importance of noninterest income are shown by the data in Table 6.1. The table shows net interest margin, noninterest income, and the percentage of noninterest income to the net interest margin at all FDIC-insured commercial banks from 1989 to 1995. The table shows the steady rise in the growth of noninterest income and as a percentage of the net interest margin. In this short, seven-year period, the percentage of noninterest income to the net interest margin rose significantly from 41.8% to 53.4%.

Table 6.1
Net Interest Income and Noninterest Income
for Insured Commercial Banks 1989–1995
(dollars in billions)

	1989	1990	1991	1992	1993	1994	1995
Net interest income ($)	112.2	115.5	121.9	133.5	139.3	146.5	154.2
Noninterest income ($)	51.1	55.1	59.7	65.6	74.9	76.3	82.4
Noninterest income/ net interest income (%)	45.5	47.7	49.0	49.1	53.8	52.1	53.4

Source: *Statistics on Banking, 1990*, Federal Deposit Insurance Corporation (Washington, D.C., 1991) and *The FDIC Quarterly Banking Profile*, Federal Deposit Insurance Corporation, various issues.

Although not shown in Table 6.1, significant increases in noninterest income have occurred at savings and loans, savings banks, and credit unions as well. In 1995, noninterest income as a percentage of the net interest margin for savings banks and savings and loans insured by the BIF was 25.1%. This is well below the comparable figures for commercial banks. The fact that thrifts are considerably more specialized than banks and have a lower percentage of liabilities in transaction accounts explains most of the difference.

The propensity to earn noninterest income differs with size. Larger institutions appear to have a far greater ability to generate noninterest income than smaller institutions. This is certainly the case for commercial banks for which data are available. Consider Table 6.2. It shows the dollar amount of noninterest income as a percentage of the bank's earning assets by size class of bank. Earning assets are those loans, leases, and security investments of banks that earn interest income. The table shows the noninterest income percentage for four size groups for the year 1994.

COSTS AND BENEFITS OF GENERATING NONINTEREST INCOME

The pursuit of noninterest-generating activities has both advantages and disadvantages. The primary advantages and disadvantages of noninterest income generating activities are discussed below.

ADVANTAGES OF NONINTEREST-GENERATING ACTIVITIES

The principal advantages relate primarily to the fact that noninterest income can usually be earned without growing the size of the balance sheet and incurring capital requirements. These and other advantages follow.

Table 6.2
Noninterest Income as a Percent of
Earning Assets by Size of Bank: 1994
(Noninterest Income ÷ Earning Assets)

Size class of banks

All banks	Less than $100 million	$100 million to $1 billion	$1 to 10 billion	Greater than $10 billion
2.27%	1.19%	1.44%	2.47%	2.67%

Source: *The FDIC Quarterly Banking Profile*, Federal Deposit Insurance Corporation. (Washington, D.C: First Quarter, 1995): p. 6.

Avoidance of Regulatory Capital Requirements

For commercial banks and thrifts the need to meet regulatory capital requirements provides a very strong inducement to increase noninterest income activities. The development in the early 1990s of risk-based capital requirements put emphasis on the on- and off-balance sheet contingent liabilities of these firms. However, these capital requirements do not relate to large origination, servicing, and data processing noninterest-generating activities that involve large commitments of human and technological resources but few on-balance sheet assets. As a result, depositories subject to risk-based capital requirements have a strong inducement to grow noninterest-income-generating activities.

Less Subject to Business Cycles

Financial institutions also pursue some noninterest income generating activities in order to reduce the firm's vulnerability to the business cycle. Business activities tied to gross volume of sales transactions do not fluctuate significantly over the course of the business cycle. Even during recessions the nominal volume of sales usually rises. This means that noninterest income activities related to payment-system services continue to increase. This tendency helps to offset the cyclical behavior of other activities of financial institutions such as lending and security issuance and sales.

Diversifies Income Sources

Financial institutions pursue noninterest income-generating activities in order to diversify. Many financial institutions are dependent on the economic conditions of particular cities, states, or regions. This makes them susceptible to recessions that may lead to increases in loan delinquencies and losses. Some noninterest-generating activities serve to offset these losses.

Allows for Cross-selling of Existing Customers

Many noninterest-generating activities serve to take advantage of existing customer relationships. A customer with an account relationship is generally easier to sell new products than a person or firm that has no relationship to the firm. This fact provides the rationale for expanding the product offering of financial firms. The concept of "one-stop financial center" is based on this rationale. Today, most commercial banks and thrifts offer a wide range of loan, deposit, security, and insurance services to their existing customers to take advantage of the cross-selling opportunities.

Takes Advantage of Economies of Scale

Certain types of origination and servicing activities seem to demonstrate significant economies of scale. This is especially evident in servicing. Credit card and mortgage loan servicing organizations seem to benefit from size. Depositories usually expand those activities that benefit from declining average cost per unit serviced, increasing economies of scale. Indeed, both the credit card and mortgage loan servicing businesses are highly concentrated.

DISADVANTAGES OF NONINTEREST-GENERATING ACTIVITIES

The principal disadvantage is that most noninterest-generating activities involve increasing the operating risk of the financial institution by adding fixed costs in the form of plant and equipment and human resources. This and other disadvantages follow.

Increases the Operating Risk of the Firm

A disadvantage of noninterest-generating activities is that they require increasing the operating risk of financial firms. This means that most of these activities require investing in plant and equipment and human resources that serve to increase the fixed cost of operating the financial firm. This involves increasing the operating risk of running the firm.

Table 6.3 shows the percentage of noninterest income to average assets and nonintererest expense to earning assets for different-sized commercial banks in 1994. The data show that the percentage of noninterest income to average assets is much higher in larger sized banks. However, it is also true that the ratio of noninterest expenses to average assets is higher for large-sized banks. This finding emphasizes the positive relationship between noninterest-generating activities and higher operating risks.

Table 6.3
Noninterest Income and Expenses as a Percent of Earning Assets
for Different Sized Commercial Banks in 1994

Size class of banks

Ratio	Less than $100 million	$100 million to $1 billion	$1 to 10 billion	Greater than $10 billion
Noninterest income ÷ earning assets	1.19%	1.44%	2.47%	2.67%
Noninterest expense ÷ earning assets	3.96	4.00	4.41	4.39

Source: *The FDIC Quarter Banking Profile*, Federal Deposit Insurance Corporation. First Quarter 1995. p. 6.

Economies of Scale May Inhibit Entry

Many noninterest-generating activities involve information-processing activities, such as servicing, which may be susceptible to economies of scale. As a result, producers that are able to produce large quantities are able to achieve lower average costs than smaller producers. This is one of the reasons why the credit card and mortgage loan servicing businesses are dominated by large firms. The servicing of credit card and home mortgage portfolios benefits from substantial economies of scale.

SOURCES OF NONINTEREST INCOME

Fee income is generated by the three information processing functions of intermediaries—origination, servicing, and brokerage. Other forms of noninterest income are also generated by the portfolio management activities. The revenues are reported as noninterest income and, in some cases, as part of the net interest margin under GAAP. The following are primary sources of fee income that relate to each of these functions.

ORIGINATION SOURCES OF FEE INCOME

The origination function is a lucrative source of fee income. Many financial institutions charge fees to customers to help offset the high costs normally attributed to the origination of financial assets. The most well known of these are underwriting fees charged by investment bankers. Most other intermediaries charge origination related fees for such loans as mortgages, business loans, and installment loans. Some of the most important fees associated with the origination function are discussed below.

- *Loan Origination:* Many types of loans involve the borrower paying an origination fee. This fee is normally assessed at the time the loan is funded. These fees are very common on real estate loans of all types including home mortgages, second mortgages, and equity lines of credit.
- *Security Underwriting:* Another form of loan origination fees are underwriting fees. Investment banks and commercial banks earn underwriting fees for the creation of securities and syndicated loans. The fees represent compensation for origination activities as well as the brokerage expertise that the institution brings to bear in order to ensure that the claim is distributed to investors.

  Until 1990, commercial bank holding companies (BHCs) were prohibited by the Federal Reserve Board (FRB) from underwriting and distributing corporate securities.[1] In 1990, the FRB provided authority to certain BHCs to underwrite and distribute corporate securities.[2]
- *Real Estate Appraisal:* Virtually all real estate loans involve the assessment of the cost of a real estate appraisal. This is by the lender's staff appraiser or an outside contract appraiser.

SERVICING SOURCES OF FEE INCOME

Servicing is a very substantial source of noninterest income for most financial institutions. Servicing activities are provided to commercial and retail customers. Generally, these services are priced using explicit fees, such as an annual fee on a credit card, or as an increment to the interest rate charged on commercial, mortgage, and installment loans. The most important servicing fee income sources include those related to investing and operations and to running the nation's payment system. These two sources are discussed below.

INVESTMENT AND OPERATIONAL SOURCES OF NONINTEREST INCOME

Financial institutions usually look for opportunities to increase revenue by selling a service they provide to their customers to other institutions that, in turn, distribute the product to their customers. Many of these services involve data processing and other asset and liability servicing functions that are offered for a fee to other institutions too small to service the product efficiently. There are a host of these "correspondent services" provided by large commercial banks and other financial institutions. Financial asset management services are offered to new and existing customers by leveraging off of the asset management skills of depositories.

- *Commercial Bank Correspondent and Data-processing Services:* Large commercial banks have historically provided a number of services for smaller commercial banks and thrifts over the years. The most important of these is check-processing services. Larger banks also process credit card receivables and other accounts for smaller financial depositories.[3] Some commercial banks also have developed computer service bureaus that provide a full range of information processing (EDP), general-ledger accounting, human resource, and payroll services for smaller institutions. Most of these servicing activities are highly automated. Very expensive proprietary software is developed by the leading firms. These firms will frequently sell or license the use of the software or process the work of other financial firms for a fee. There are hundreds of different types of services financial institutions perform for each other. These can be priced explicitly for each service or the services can be bundled and a single fee can be assessed.

The most common data processing services include checking account, savings account, credit card, mortgage loan, general ledger, payroll, and commercial and industrial loan processing.

- *Security Transfer and Registration:* Small numbers of commercial banks are active in the data-processing activities required in the stock transfer and registration of securities. These banks generate significant revenue from this noninterest-generating activity.
- *Trust Services:* Providing trust services is an important revenue source for a number of financial institutions. This activity involves managing a client's financial and real assets. The trust entity normally provides safekeeping, advisory, accounting, record keeping, and management services for the client. Trust fees are normally assessed on the amount of assets under management. Trust services are considered by a number of bankers to have significant long-term potential. The asset management business, especially that of mutual funds, has grown rapidly in the last decade.
- *Portfolio Management Services:* Mutual fund asset managers, managers of real estate investment trusts, general partners in limited partnerships, and specialized asset management companies derive their revenue from pure portfolio management services. These organizations and individuals, like the trust companies, manage assets for a fee. Many larger financial institutions provide asset management services through subsidiaries.

- *Credit and Debit Card Annual Maintenance Services:* Most providers of credit and debit cards charge an annual maintenance fee to offset the cost of account servicing.
- *Mortgage Servicing* : A mortgage sold in the secondary market is serviced by the seller or another agent. This activity involves collection, statement production, payoff handling, and processing delinquencies and foreclosures. It is typical for the servicer to earn an annualized fee of 25 to 50 basis points on the outstanding loan balance. A number of large financial institutions have mortgage banking subsidiaries that specialize in the servicing of mortgages in order to generate mortgage servicing fee income.
- *Corporate Loan Syndication and Participation Servicing:* Large corporate loans are frequently sold, in whole or in part, to other lenders in the form of a syndication or participation. The originating institution, or lead lender, may sell off one or more participations in the loan to other lenders. The lead institution will earn a servicing fee by selling the loan to another lender at an interest rate that is somewhat below the loan contractual rate paid by the borrower. This creates servicing income for the selling institution.

SERVICING FEES THAT ARE TRANSACTION-RELATED

Financial institutions operate the nation's payment system. The cost of operating the payment system involves the assessment of many fees to users of the system. Depositories are the major recipient of these fees. Some of the most important include those discussed below.

- *Credit and Debit Card Transaction Servicing:* Credit and debit card issuers earn transaction income related to the use of the card. Financial institutions earn a fee from the merchant that accepts the card. This fee is split two ways. A portion goes to the card-issuing institution and a portion goes to the institution that converts the card receipts to cash for the merchant (merchant fee).
- *Checking Account Servicing:* Financial institutions earn a number of different types of fees on checking accounts. They include monthly maintenance fees, per-check use fees, nonsufficient funds (NSF) fees, and other fees for assisting the customer in using and maintaining the account.
- *Lock-Box Services:* The lock-box is a service involving mail-receiving boxes. Financial institutions that provide this service have local payment-processing centers that ensure the timely receipt of checks and timely depositing into the receiving firm's account. This cash management service assists the firm in minimizing its float.
- *Cash Management Services:* Related to lock-box services is a full range of cash management services offered primarily by commercial banks. These services include such activities as accounts receivable collection, payment of accounts payable, investment of excess liquidity, and developing pro-forma cash flow statements.

- *Automated Transaction Machine Services:* Many financial institutions offer automated transaction services through automated transaction machines (ATMs) and earn fees.
- *Computerized Banking and Brokerage Services:* Although relatively new, computerized banking and brokerage are now being offered. These services allow the customer to review account balances, shift funds between accounts, implement security purchases and sales, and access an array of informational services.

BROKERAGE SOURCES OF FEE INCOME

Brokerage activities provide more fee-generating sources for financial institutions. Large commercial banks rely on brokerage for varying percentages of total revenue. The variety of brokerage income sources is discussed below.

- *Correspondent Brokerage Services:* Included in the services larger commercial banks provide for smaller institutions are brokerage services. Larger banks with security and foreign exchange trading departments provide security and foreign exchange purchase and sale services, as well as the safekeeping of securities, for smaller banks and thrifts. Larger banks also act as brokers, arranging for purchases and sales of Fed funds, between depositories.
- *Security Brokerage Services:* BHCs and thrift holding companies provide security brokerage services to commercial customers and consumers. The primary revenue from this activity is the brokerage commission associated with each transaction.
- *Foreign Exchange Brokerage and Advisory Services:* Financial intermediaries provide foreign exchange services to their clients. This involves buying and selling foreign currencies that earn brokerage income.
- *Insurance Brokerage Services:* Many depositories sell insurance. This includes property and casualty, mortgage life insurance, other credit insurance, and term, whole life, and investment-oriented life insurance. The income from this activity are insurance commissions. The pure brokerage of insurance is not available to all financial institutions. Since 1967, federally chartered savings and loans have been able to broker commercial property and casualty and life insurance through subsidiaries. Although BHCs can offer credit life insurance to customers because this insurance has been determined to be closely relate to banking by the Federal Reserve, legislation still prohibits the sale of most insurance by BHCs with assets over $50 million.

Insurance sales today are also a major activity for many retail broker-dealers. Insurance policies with a major investment element, such as variable rate policies and single-premium annuities, are typically sold by licensed security brokers who also obtain an insurance license to market insurance to their customers.

- *Interest Rate Swap Brokerage:* Large commercial banks act as a broker for arranging interest rate and foreign currency swaps between two parties. These brokerage activities generate income that is usually the difference between what the two parties pay the broker institution and the lesser amount the broker institution remits on to the other party. This income is pure "brokerage" income so long as the broker institution does not accept any risk due to defaulting counterparties.

PORTFOLIO MANAGEMENT FEE SOURCES

Although portfolio management activities are usually accounted for by interest income and expense, accounting conventions don't always provide for accounting for it this way. There are several activities of financial institutions that require portfolio risk management that earn revenues that are typically not included in interest income. These are discussed below.

- *Loan Commitments:* Loan commitments are issued by most financial institutions involved in portfolio management activities. A loan commitment is a legally binding contract between a lender and borrower that specifies the amount of funds, time period, and price for a loan to be taken down in the forward market. Five common uses of loan commitments include:

  1. A mortgage borrower is preparing to purchase a house and desires to obtain the promise of a loan now (called a mortgage loan commitment) even though closing of the transaction will be several months in the future.
  2. A corporate issuer of commercial paper (called a standby letter of credit) wants to have a backup source of short-term financing should the commercial paper market become unsettled and the firm finds it difficult to roll over the paper.
  3. A builder-developer is looking for a short-term mortgage (called real estate takeout commitment) to ensure that a temporary form of permanent financing is available when the real estate project is completed.
  4. A corporate borrower engaged in a business acquisition (called a credit letter of intent) wants to prove to the management and directors of the target company that it has sufficient funds lined up to complete the transaction.
  5. A corporation or foreign government obtains a line of credit for several years to ensure it will be able to sell its short-term securities in the open market and, if not, be assured that the lender will guarantee to purchase the securities (called a note issuance facility).

To the borrower, a loan commitment represents a form of guarantee that financing will be available to meet an offsetting obligation. This makes the loan commitment a form of insurance. For other types of insurance, the insured would expect to pay a premium. It is no different for a loan commitment. The difference is that in lending business the fee is called a loan commitment fee. The amount of the fee is negotiated between borrower and lender.

- *Loan Guarantees:* Occasionally, a financial institution will guarantee the timely payment of principal and interest on notes or securities issued by a third party. The third party usually has a low credit rating and without the guarantee would be forced to pay a higher interest rate. The guarantor institution must view the guarantee as part of the credit risk it maintains in its portfolio even though the guarantee does not show up on the balance sheet. The guarantor institution will typically be paid a fee for providing the guarantee.

- *Acting as Principal in Swaps:* Commercial banks are active as participants in currency and interest rate swaps. These transactions do not show up on the balance sheet but do involve credit, interest rate, and settlement risks. As a principal in a swap transaction, the financial institution will earn a fee usually priced as a percent of the notional principal of the swap.

SUMMARY

Given the ongoing pressures on the net interest margin of depositories, noninterest income has become increasingly important for these firms. Origination, servicing, and brokerage are major sources of noninterest income for depositories.

Much of the income generated by these sources is included in the interest rate earned on the assets held in portfolio. The portion that is earned explicitly is now over 50% of the net interest income of commercial banks and over 20% for thrifts. Most of this income is fee income charged borrowers, income earned for servicing assets for third parties, and fees related to transaction processing.

The portfolio management activities of depositories also earn noninterest income. This income is derived from loan commitments and guarantees offered by these institutions.

NOTES

1. BHCs had been granted the approval to underwrite state and local municipal bonds and asset-backed securities in 1987. The Fed required that these activities be conducted through nonbank subsidiaries.

2. The first BHC to receive the Fed-granted authority was J. P. Morgan & Co.

3. The most important correspondent services provided by large commercial banks correspondents include check clearing, data processing, short-term credit lines, and security brokerage.

Chapter 7 . . . .

Product-Line Performance Appraisal Systems Introduction

INTRODUCTION

The secular decline in profitability at depositories has only recently been broken, for commercial banks at least, by the sharp reduction in the number of depositories and by a record postwar decline in short-term interest rates, which raised interest rate margins in the early 1990s. The causes of these long-term profit pressures have not gone away. Increased global competition, deregulation, and technological advances are all serving to reduce profit margins in the basic product offered by depositories. These ongoing pressures on profit margins make it necessary for depositories to improve their management performance assessment tools.

The performance appraisal models presented in this chapter are such tools. Here, profitability systems are developed for each processing function (especially origination and servicing) performed by depositories along with a practical methodology for collecting and organizing the necessary data.

The fundamental feature of the performance appraisal models presented is the recognition that depositories can unbundle the processing functions they perform for each asset and liability. This is done by using the system of unbundling discussed in Chapter 3.

MODELS OF INTERMEDIARY COSTS AND REVENUES BY FUNCTION

Under GAAP, the income statements of intermediaries are not unbundled. This does not mean that a conceptual redesign of the income statement cannot be developed for enhanced management control and reporting purposes. This is done by unbundling the various functions of the intermediary and demonstrating how each of these functions generates its own revenues and costs. Equation 7.1 defines the intermediary's total profit.

Total profit before tax *(TP)* = Net origination income *(NOI)*
+ Net servicing income *(NSI)*
+ Net brokerage income *(NBI)*
+ Net portfolio income *(NPI)*   [7.1]

NET ORIGINATION INCOME

The loan origination unit's function is to work with the borrowers of the assets it originates to create desirable loans profitably and with savers to create desirable liability products. The origination unit must originate assets with specific risk and return parameters to meet the needs of the depository's own portfolio manager or a secondary market purchaser. The liabilities originated must also meet the needs of the portfolio manager in terms of price, maturity, and cost of servicing.

The origination unit's revenue is derived from three sources: (1) explicit fees charged the borrower or saver; (2) internal transfers based on contractual agreements with the firm's portfolio management unit; and (3) explicit profit from sales of assets to secondary market investors. Unfortunately, many assets and liabilities are originated without collecting explicit revenues needed to cover the costs of performing the origination function. Management can think of many products it originates that do not generate explicit fee charged to the customer such as auto loans, credit card receivables, savings and transaction accounts, some mortgage loans, and some business loans. Imagine asking a depositor to pay a 1 percent fee to cover the cost of opening a new account. Some loans do involve charging explicit origination fees, but frequently those fees are inadequate to cover the costs of origination. In many cases the fees charged do not relate to the actual cost of origination but relate to prevailing industry practice.

Determining the revenue for each asset and liability origination unit involves determining the appropriate revenue streams for each. As discussed above, there are three sources of revenue associated with performing origination services. Some origination units also sell their underwriting and investment expertise. One example of this revenue source is fees earned by the firm selling whole loans, securities, or loan participations or syndications to third-party investors at higher prices than the cost of obtaining them at origination.

If assets or liabilities can be originated by a third party at a cost lower (or higher) than the explicit fees, plus agreed-upon internally transferred contractual fees, plus any marketing gains or losses, then the difference is profit (or loss) to the origination unit. This profit or loss represents a financial measure of the performance of each origination group within the firm.

The unit's origination income statement will look like Equation 7.2.

NOI = Origination revenue (Ro) less Origination costs (Co)   [7.2]
where:

$Ro = \sum^{n}_{i\ =\ 1} [(A_i\ F_i) - C_i\ ]$ = Origination revenue consisting of explicit origination fees charged the customer, internal transfer fees charged to the firm's portfolio, plus gain or loss on the sale of the asset if sold in the secondary market of amount A_i times fee F_i for a total of n claims originated less the cost of origination C_i

A_i = Asset i represented in dollars

F_i = Fee i represented as a percent of A_i

C_i = Costs of origination for asset i

An example of computing NOI would be a business loan originating unit of a hypothetical XYZ Commercial Bank that originates $42 million of loans in a year and receives a 1 percent origination fee. The 1 percent origination fee is determined by management as an internal transfer price and is based on market data. That is, the origination fee credited the origination unit is based on the prices charged for comparable services available from third-party originators, such as loan brokers or other banks.

The theory is that the internal unit should be as efficient as outside third-party competitors. The portfolio manager can usually buy assets in the secondary market similar to the ones originated. Assets purchased in the secondary market would involve the payment of an origination fee, in the form either of an explicit fee or the loss of a certain amount of interest measured as the difference between the yield on the originated loan versus the interest earned on a similar loan purchased in the secondary market. If the unit's cost of operations was $400,000 per year, the unit's profit would be [$42,000,000 ($A_i$) * .01 ($F_i$) - $400,000 ($C_i$) =] $20,000.

Consider another example. The firm originates home mortgages, or alternatively can buy them wholesale from a mortgage broker. The origination fee charged the borrower are the same for mortgages originated versus those obtained from the broker. The cost of originating loans in the volume needed is $1,450,000 ($1,250,000 direct and $200,000 indirect costs). The origination fees earned on the target $350,000,000 in loans scheduled to be put in portfolio is (.01 * $350,000 =) $350,000. The loans originated have a coupon rate of 8.00 percent, which includes the cost of servicing. If the firm purchases the loans from the broker, it will pay a premium price, earn no fees, and achieve a return of 7.95%. It would cost the firm $100,000 to operate a wholesale mortgage acquisition department. The portfolio manager has determined that the yield of 7.95%, which includes the cost of servicing, will meet the portfolio's required target yield.

If the firm originates in-house, it will earn the additional (8.00% - 7.95% =) 5 basis points. Based on the most realistic prepayment forecast, this interest strip is expected to be worth a present value of .30% of the value of the mortgages originated in house. This additional yield belongs to the origination unit since the additional value of these mortgages is related to the fact that they are originated in house. Adding the additional .30% as an internal transfer from the portfolio yield to the origination unit results in a total revenue of $350,000 in explicit fees plus (.30% * $350,000,000 =) $1,050,000.

The product-line income statement for the origination unit is shown in Table 7.1.

Table 7.1
Annual Pro-Forma Income Statement for XYZ Bank
In-House Mortgage Origination Unit

Revenue:	
Explicit fees charged customers	$350,000
Internal transfer fees charged to portfolio	1,050,000
Gain (or loss) on marketing loans to third parties	0
Total revenue	$1,400,000
Costs:	
Direct costs	$1,250,000
Indirect costs	200,000
Total costs	
Pretax profit (or loss)	($50,000)

Comparing the cost of obtaining $350,000,000 in loans with a net yield of 7.95 percent for the portfolio would result in either: (1) a net cost of $100,000 using the broker; or (2) a loss profit of ($350,000 + $1,050,000 - $1,450,000 =) -$50,000 using the in-house origination unit. Given these alternatives, the in-house unit is the least-cost alternative. However, management must still deal with the fact that the origination office faces a loss.

From the firm's portfolio manager's perspective, a portion of the interest on many loans brought into portfolio is really compensation for work performed by the origination unit. As the next section will show, an additional portion of the interest earned represents revenues that really belong to the servicing unit within the firm.

NET SERVICING INCOME

The depository's servicing units also act as contract agents for the portfolio manager and any outside institutions that invest in assets serviced by it. All financial claims must be serviced. Consequently, the intermediary must determine who will service each claim it holds in portfolio. Servicing is done by the firm itself or contractually by a third party.

A commercial bank syndicating a commercial term loan, for example, has to obtain a price from the servicing unit for the in-house servicing activities it performs for outside investors. Alternatively, the portfolio manager can find an outside servicer who might be able to service for less than the in-house unit. If so, the transfer price paid by the portfolio unit to the in-house servicing unit should be the lower price offered by the outside third-party servicer. If the in-house servicing unit is particularly efficient, it will be able to service at a price below the contract price. This creates profit for the servicing unit.

The income statement of the servicing unit for each asset and liability serviced is shown as Equation 7.3.

$$NSI = \sum^n_{i=1} \text{[Revenue from servicing fees (transfer prices) paid by the portfolio or outside investors (explicit revenues) for each firm } i \ (Rs_i)$$

less Servicing costs for servicing for each firm i (Cs_i) [7.3]

where:
   i = Servicing for firm i.
   n = Number of firms serviced for

Consider Mainline Commercial Bank selling syndications on $80 million of loans. It services the loans for a fee of .25 percent of the principal balance per annum. If it costs the servicing unit $170,000 per year in operating direct and indirect costs, its profit from servicing would be ($80,000,000 * .0025 - $170,000 =) $30,000.

A more complicated example would be a mortgage lending thrift that has an active secondary market mortgage sales program. This institution holds $120,000,000 in mortgages in its own portfolio and has sold and currently services $450,000,000 in mortgage principal of loans sold to Fannie Mae and Freddie Mac. The firm earns .375 percent annually on the loans sold in the secondary market. This is considered an appropriate market price which the firm could obtain if the servicing was performed by a third-party servicer. The portfolio manager has determined that an internal transfer price of .375 percent annually is also appropriate on the loans held in portfolio. The cost of operating the servicing unit is $1,900,000 of direct and $150,000 of indirect costs. The unit's income statement would look like Table 7.2.

Each servicing unit within the firm must negotiate servicing fees for each asset and liability. These fees should be based on fee levels charged by third-party providers of the service so that the in-house servicer's performance is evaluated against a market standard. Many institutions make the mistake of negotiating transfer prices based on the costs of the unit providing the service. All this does is institutionalize inefficiency if the in-house unit is not effective. Where there are no comparable third-party providers of the service, the negotiation of fees is decidedly more difficult. In this case, it is worthwhile to use data from peer groups or trade associations.

Table 7.2
Product-Line Statement for In-House Servicing Unit
(annualized)

Revenue:	
Fees earned from in-house portfolio manager	$450,000
Fees earned from outside investors	1,687,500
Total revenue:	2,137,500
Direct costs	1,900,000
Indirect costs	150,000
Total costs	2,050,000
Pretax profit (or loss)	$87,500

NET BROKERAGE INCOME

Brokerage income from third-party brokerage is generally easy to measure. This revenue is simply the difference between what the brokerage function is able to obtain as a commission, defined as the difference between the price received by the seller, and the price paid by the buyer.

The broker's income statement would look like Equation 7.4.

$$NBI = (Rb_i) \text{ less Cost of operating the brokerage unit } (Cb) \qquad [7.4]$$

where:

$Rb = \sum^n_{i=1}$ [Price of claim i bought from a third party (Ps_i) less Price of claim i sold to a third party (Pb_i)]

n = Number of brokerage transactions

An example would be the discount-fee security brokerage subsidy of XYZ Commercial Bank that brokers 10,000,000 shares of stock per year at an average commission rate of $.30 per share. If this firm had a cost of $2,900,000 per annum, its profit would be (10,000,000 * $.30 - $2,900,000 =) $100,000.

NET PORTFOLIO INCOME

Portfolio income is measured solely on the performance of the portfolio in terms of net interest margin on loans and securities held in portfolio, trading gains or losses on loans and securities sold, and any fees earned on guarantees made and commitments that result in contingent liabilities for the portfolio. The portfolio manager must manage interest rate risk, credit risk, and liquidity risk. The contribution of the portfolio manager is normally measured by the net interest margin. However, fees paid for origination, servicing, and brokerage are subtracted from the portfolio's income.

A portfolio management unit's income statement is shown in Equation 7.5.

NPI = Portfolio income from interest and gain and loss on sale of assets (R_p) less Portfolio interest paid on liabilities and cost of capital to support assets held (I_p) less Cost of portfolio management services (Cp) less Loan losses (L_a) less Fees charged by origination units for their services(R_o) less Fees charged by servicing units for their services (R_s)   [7.5]

An example is XYZ Commercial Bank with interest income and gain on sale of securities of $120,000,000 in 19XY. Its interest costs are $115,000,000 per annum. The firm pays their own or a third-party origination unit a fee of 1 percent of the unpaid principal of the loans that are put in the firm's portfolio. In 19XY, $42,000,000 in loans were originated for the portfolio at a fee of 1 percent of principal. The servicing unit services $200,000,000 of loans for the portfolio and $80,000,000 in commercial loans for correspondents. It has negotiated a fee, or internal transfer price, of .20 percent of the principal dollar amount of loans serviced and receives .25 percent on servicing for correspondents. The institution suffers loan losses $65,000 during the year. The cost of operating the portfolio management unit is $234,000. XYZ Commercial Bank's portfolio income statement would look like Table 7.3 when displayed using GAAP.

A review of any depository's income statement would reveal that the interest margin from the portfolio and noninterest income generated from origination, brokerage, and servicing are all major components. The revenues and costs shown here are accounted for differently under GAAP from that proposed under the product-line performance system because in most depositories the functions are combined under GAAP. The GAAP approach makes it impossible to determine the performance of each function performed. Moreover, most firms do not have the data retrieval system to capture the appropriate functional performance data, although many firms are developing this capability.

PRODUCT-LINE INCOME AND LOSS STATEMENTS

As we have seen, depositories generate income from their origination, servicing, brokerage, and portfolio management activities. Table 7.3 reclassifies the income and expense to coincide with each financial product and function performed. Although Table 7.3 shows origination, servicing, and brokerage for only one type of financial claim, in reality all the major assets and liabilities of the firm would have separate income and expense statements. The need for product-line income and loss statements is reflected by the growing importance of origination, brokerage, and servicing income at commercial banks.

The most difficult job in creating product-line income and expense reports is determining the appropriate estimates of the revenues and costs. Many administrative and support expenses are difficult to allocate to business lines.

This process necessitates a negotiation process between staff overhead units and those that are in the product-line functions. The primary administrative and support functions that are typically allocated include:

- accounting
- executive management
- human resources
- legal
- corporate internal and external audit
- corporate marketing
- training
- public and shareholder relations

Table 7.3
XYZ Commercial Bank Income Statement

Interest income (R_p)		$120,000,000
Interest expense (I_p)		115,000,000
Net interest margin		$5,000,000
Noninterest income:		
Origination (R_o)	$420,000	
Servicing) (Rs_i)	200,000	
Brokerage (Rb)	3,000,000	
Total noninterest income:		3,620,000
Expenses of portfolio management unit (C_p)	-$234,000	
Less cost of origination (C_o)	-400,000	
Cost of servicing (C_{si})	-170,000	
Brokerage costs (Cb)	-2,900,000	
Total noninterest expenses		-3,754,000
Net profit before taxes and loan losses		$4,866,000
Loan loss provisions (L_a)		65,000
Portfolio income (pre-tax)		$4,801,000

The proper negotiation process involves allocating 100 percent of the corporate overhead expenses to each of the functional business lines. In determining the transfer prices used to allocate fees from one functional unit to another, it is important to use third-party market prices rather than internally generated transfer prices. If your origination unit is unusually inefficient, you build in an artificially high transfer price if you use their costs to determine the transfer price. Find out what a third party would charge for origination and servicing and use those prices as transfer prices. The objective is to have your origination units competing with third-party originators. Product-line statements are also produced for liabilities issued by depositories. This methodology is covered in Chapter 8.

The other important requirement discussed in Chapter 4 is that all costs must be allocated, including the cost of the board of directors. Corporate cost centers not allocated to revenue-producing units will soon turn into a huge unallocated pot if the operating units have their way.

Even more difficult than the allocation of expenses is the allocation of income. In this functional product-line system, the portfolio management function is clearly differentiated from the origination, servicing, and brokerage functions. This is a critical separation, since it makes clear the fact that origination and servicing activities do not receive revenue related to the ongoing interest and capital gain (losses) related to assets held in portfolio. Rather, the origination units receive revenue related to an agreed-upon amount from the loan investor for performing the origination activity. The servicer likewise receives a negotiated amount for performing servicing. The buyer of the loan, whether it be the firm's portfolio or third-party secondary market organization, will pay the fees out of the portfolio revenues they expect to earn. However, the fees are calculated as an up front payment accrued at the time a loan is delivered to the buyer.[1]

USING THE MODEL FOR PERFORMANCE APPRAISAL: RETURN ON EQUITY

Most depositories are involved in multiple origination, servicing, and brokerage activities as well as portfolio management. GAAP accounting statements aggregate their revenue and cost data in such a way as to make it impossible to use them for performance appraisal by individual functional units within the firm. For example, just such a system is necessary to determine whether management should invest additional capital into a mortgage servicing activity as compared to increasing the size of the business loan origination unit.

The key to assessing the performance of these functional product lines is to categorize the revenue and expenses data of the firm in such a way that they can be properly attributed to each product line, as shown in Table 7.4, and then to divide the income after tax by the equity required to support that function. This is possible using the functional breakdown discussed in the previous two sections.

Determining the amount of the firm's equity to allocate to each function is not a straightforward problem. Equity to support the portfolio management function is estimated by using something like the regulator's risk-based asset capital requirements for both credit and interest rate risks. The minimum amount can be modified by management to adjust to the firm's optimal capital structure. The capital to be allocated to origination, servicing, and brokerage is not nearly as easy to estimate. The best method to determine the appropriate capital level for operating units is to use a capital level based on that of competitors who operate "functionally pure" firms such as stand-alone brokers, loan servicers, or loan originators. A second method is to use physical assets plus a specified number of months of average personnel and space costs. This amount is used because this number represents a good estimate of the operating risk of the unit. If the unit were shut down, the firm would have to bear the costs of shutdown. Management must consider whether this approach is reasonable for each operating unit. The returns on equity (ROE) are estimated for XYZ Commercial Bank in Table 7.5.

The resulting product-line ROE statement allows management to assess each operating unit within the firm. Its strength is that each unit is evaluated for only those activities and decisions over which it has control. The system also eliminates the common problem where operating units are penalized or rewarded for actions and decisions of others.

Table 7.4
Product-Line Income and Expense Statement

Income and expense category	Portfolio management	Origination unit	Servicing unit	Brokerage unit
Interest income	$119,180,000			
Interest expense	115,000,000			
Loan loss reserves	65,000			
Net interest margin	4,115,000			
Noninterest income				
Unit income		$420,000	$600,000	$3,000,000
Unit expense	234,000	400,000	170,000	2,900,000
Before-tax profit	3,881,000	$20,000	$430,000	$100,000
Taxes @35%	1,358,350	7,000	150,500	35,000
After-tax profit	$2,522,650	$13,000	$279,500	$65,000

In the increasingly competitive financial markets, depository managements must have the tools to know which functions their firms perform profitably.

The problem is that the financial records of depositories are not conducive to making these assessments. By developing product-line income statements, it is possible to provide performance reports that accurately measure the value added for each of the origination, servicing, and brokerage units within the firm and separately for the intermediation function, the portfolio.

Table 7.5
Estimated Return on Equity for Functions Performed by
XYZ Commercial Bank

	Portfolio Management	Origination	Servicing	Brokerage
After-tax profit	$2,522,650	$13,000	$279,500	$65,000
Equity required to support unit	$18,000,000	$1,500,000	$700,000	$500,000
Return on equity	14.01%	.87%	39.93%	13.00%

SUMMARY

This chapter provides the specifics for developing product-line performance systems for origination, servicing, brokerage, and portfolio management activities for depository firms.

In order to develop these systems it is necessary to identify and measure sources of direct and indirect revenues and costs for each origination, servicing, and brokerage unit. Once these revenues and costs are developed, a simple income and loss statement can be developed for each profit center.

NOTE

1. In the product-line performance system for originators, the origination fees, both explicit and transfer revenues, are not amortized as they sometimes are under GAAP. Revenues and costs are accounted for at the time of the transaction.

Chapter 8 . . . .

Measuring Retail Depository Branch Performance

INTRODUCTION

The purpose of this chapter is to develop a theoretically sound and practical way for depositories to measure the profitability of deposit-gathering branch offices. The focus here is on the liability side of the balance sheet, especially that related to attracting retail deposits. Depositories have invested billions of dollars in brick-and-mortar facilities, data-processing systems, and personnel to operate branch offices used to originate and service liabilities and distribute other financial products. Also discussed is a branch personnel incentive program which is consistent with our model of branch profit measurement.

The need for branch profitability measures is obvious given the large number of branches and personnel who work in them. Exhibit 8.1 shows the number of banks and branches of FDIC-insured commercial banks and trusts from 1959 through 1993. Note that while there has been a pronounced reduction in the number of banks in the 1990s, there continues to be a large increase in branch offices. The increase in branch offices is primarily the result of commercial bank acquisitions of weak and failed savings and loans.

WHY A BRANCH PROFITABILITY MODEL IS NEEDED

The need to accurately measure the profit contribution of a branch is greater today than ever before. Consider the following six reasons. First, the deregulation of the deposit-rate ceilings has made the cost of retail deposit gathering from commercial branches more expensive.

Second, the deregulation of deposit rates has forced a change in the competitive service mix. In the days of Regulation Q, depositories competed with convenience such as many offices, free services, and a physiological feeling of safety that manifested itself as large, costly permanent facilities. Competing on the basis of interest rate or price was prohibited. All institutions need to evaluate the profitability of their branch networks.

Exhibit 8.1
FDIC-Insured Banks and Offices 1959–1993

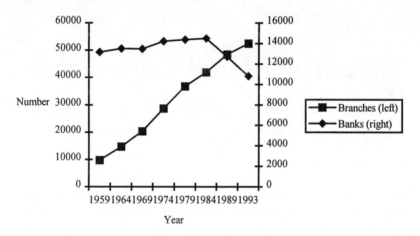

Source: *1993 Statistics on Banking*, Federal Deposit Insurance Corporation, Washington DC, 1994.

Third, the Financial Institution Reform Recovery and Enforcement Act of 1989 has resulted in thousands of branch offices being offered for sale by the Resolution Trust Corporation and FDIC. The RTC aggressively sold many of the offices of institutions that have gone into receivership. Institutions wanting to bid on them will need to value these branches.

Fourth, measuring branch profitability is necessary because of the growth and availability of other types of assured deposit distribution channels.

Fifth, there is an established trend among insured depositories to buy, sell, and trade existing facilities. The feeling is that in many markets consolidation is necessary to restore and enhance profitability. Knowing the value of each branch you own and being able to value those offered to you is a necessary skill.

Finally, a branch profitability measurement system assists in developing a branch personnel compensation incentive system that encourages behavior that is consistent in its profit measurement objectives.

MODEL OF BRANCH FUNCTIONS AND ACTIVITIES

Central to the development of the branch model are two critical assumptions. The first is that the depository's investment decisions be evaluated independently of the firm's funding alternatives. This assumption is very important since the performance of units within the intermediary responsible for originating assets and investing funds should not be affected by good or bad performance by the branches in attracting deposits.

Conversely, the management responsible for the retail branch system should not have their performance affected because the assets acquired with the deposits performed better or worse than expected because of economic volatility. Branches are not responsible for the portfolio management decisions of depository intermediaries.

The second assumption is that the retail branch should be looked at fundamentally as a distribution system for financial products and services. In this respect, it is no different from a retail store selling soft goods. Norwest Corporation out of Minneapolis is one of the nation's strongest advocates of the retail financial store concept. This bank holding company with over $55 billion in assets at year-end 1994 refers to its retail deposit branches and mortgage bank origination offices as "stores." In their 1994 annual report they wrote the following. "We're a national financial services company. We're a sales and service business. A sales per square foot business. We measure our stores' performance on sales growth. The number of bank products sold per household. Originations per Norwest Mortgage store."[1]

Virtually all products and services of a depository delivered through a retail branch are today successfully distributed using a variety of alternative distribution channels. Some, like credit cards, are more successfully delivered through direct mail than through retail branches. Consequently, the retail branch is simply one of many alternative distribution channels available to the depository.

With these two assumptions understood, we are able to define the functions of a retail branch and develop the branch's revenue and cost cash flows. To do this, the functions of a branch must first be carefully unbundled.

At this point, we should point out that a number of depositories use an alternative branch model of profitability and return on equity. This model makes an alternative assumption concerning the functions of the branch. Rather than viewing the branch as a component of the firm's distribution system, this alternative views the branch as similar to a stand-alone independent intermediary. In this alternative framework, the branch originates, services, and invests in loans as well as offering deposit services.

Institutions that view their branches in this manner must create an income statement that includes the interest revenue, less loan losses, on the loans originated by the branch from which all the costs used in our model are taken. This approach also involves an allocation for interest revenue on loans not originated by the branch that represent the difference between the deposits of the branch and the loans it originates, if branch deposits exceed loans. This alternative also requires calculating a capital contribution based on the amount of equity the firm must supply to support the assets and liabilities of the branch. This equity allocation permits the calculation of return on equity for the branch.

There are several reasons why this approach is rejected. First, the people running the branch are typically not involved in determining the products offered by the depository, the prices charged, or any of the other portfolio management issues that impact on the transfer prices used for calculating asset revenues and liability costs. Second, the primary role of the branch is servicing existing accounts and selling additional products. Since these are the responsibilities of the branch, it is important that the performance system used precisely measure the quality of its sales efforts and servicing efficiency. This is not the case with the alternative method.

This system views the branch in the more limited role as part of the firm's distribution network. Here branch personnel are not responsible for portfolio management and loan pricing. It also assumes that the deposits generated by the branch are simply substitutes for other sources of loanable funds. Thus, the notion that branches are semi-independent institutions is rejected.

This system views the major functions of the branch to be the origination and servicing of various asset and liability products of the firm. However, because of the substantially different operating strategies used by financial depositories around the country, each institution must perform this analysis for itself. The system defines the activities associated with origination to be the preparing of documents for deposit accounts and loans. Branch personnel may also be involved in a complete or partial underwriting or credit scoring activity. Some depositories delegate branches complete underwriting in the branch as well as funding the loan. Still, others use the branch as simply a distribution channel, with the branch personnel acting as a direct sales force, but not a loan processing or underwriting unit.

The servicing activities of the branch relate to the activities of payment processing, deposit processing, and transaction processing to the extent these activities occur within the branch. The branches of some institutions might also serve to distribute products and services not produced by the firm. In this case, we must measure the commission or service fee cash flows derived through the sale of loans (underwritten and funded elsewhere in the institution), safety deposit boxes, mutual fund, insurance, and agent-based credit card programs.

CROSS-SELLING REVENUES

In many depository institutions the branch personnel sell a variety of products, but do not perform the origination or servicing on them. Rather they act as agent for origination units within the firm that complete the transaction after the agent provides a lead or application. This activity is referred to as cross-selling.

How much revenue the branch should get to act as an agent is necessarily negotiable with the origination units. If the branch brings in good prospects for a loan, credit card, or insurance product, the origination units should be willing to offer a portion of the origination fee they earn. This amount becomes a portion of the revenue for the branch.

The beauty of using the agent-revenue approach is that the branch personnel can focus on those products that maximize the revenue and, therefore, profits for the branch rather than meeting the sometimes arbitrary targets or goals set by the home office. The branch personnel feel as if they are in control of their own destiny.

LET EACH BRANCH PROMOTE THE BEST-SELLING PRODUCTS AND SERVICES

One of the greatest failings of many depositories is attempting to launch product promotions from the main office. Today's large multistate holding companies have branches located in markets that differ significantly from one another. The key to developing a sales organization is to give the branch "sales" manager and front-line employees the products and services they need to meet the needs of the local community and its existing customer base. This means that not all branches will want to promote the same products or will want to promote their products at the same time during the year.

Using this chapter's model of branch profitability, each office can be given considerable latitude to market those products and services that are demanded by their customer base are most profitable as reflected on the branch's profit and loss statement.

Allowing branches to manage a portion of the firm's promotion and advertising budget is possible using a program called "Locally Executed Advertising and Promotion" (LEAP). This program is designed to encourage and assist branches in executing product and service promotions within their local communities and neighborhoods. Chapter 11 describes the program and includes some material used to implement it. Included in the chapter is a discussion of the role of local promotions, a method of planning for the return on investment from a promotion program, and systematic method for planning a promotion.

MEASUREMENT MODEL OF BRANCH PROFITABILITY

With this model of the functions of the branch developed, this firm is able to specify the profit and loss model for the branch. The model for the income statement is total branch profits (TBP) equals branch servicing income (BSI), plus branch origination income (BOI), plus branch fee and commission income (BFC), minus branch total costs (BTC).

Branch servicing fee income (BSI) includes an allocation provided the branch from any servicing groups within the firm that receive services performed by branch personnel such as loan posting, payment processing, and collection. A branch that collects and posts loan payments for mortgages may receive a revenue allocation of $.25 per payment, for example. Since many branches are not involved in this type of activity, they may earn no servicing income.

Branch origination income (*BOI*) is the largest and most important source of income for most branches. Origination income cash flows come in two forms. The first source relates to financial products and services the branch successfully markets to the public on behalf of the firm's asset managers. Asset managers can be thought of as product managers who have the responsibility to market specific loans or other financial service products. These product managers look at the branch as one of several alternative distribution channels available to them.

Here the branch should be allocated revenue based on what the asset or loan manager feels it can pay to obtain additional sales of the product. The revenue is in the form of commissions, e.g., $12 per credit card issued, .25 percent of the funded dollar amount of any first or second mortgage originated through the branch, and so forth. Each loan and service sales unit that wants to use the branch to distribute product must determine what type of commission and processing fee it can afford to pay the branch to market its product.

The second form of *BOI* relates to the sale of deposit products. This is by far the most important source of income for virtually all retail depository branches. This income is derived by remembering that the branch-generated retail deposit is but one of a number of alternative funding sources for the firm. Consequently, the asset and liability managers of the firm should be constantly monitoring prices for all alternative funding sources. These prices, along with monitoring the competition, form the basis of the pricing used by the retail branch system.

This analysis also forms the basis for developing the cash flows for the branch relating to deposit acquisition. These cash flows are based on the assumption that the goal of the branch is to maximize the present value of the difference between the marginal cost of raising funds through the branch compared to the next least cost alternative for raising funds through other distribution channels. These alternative sources of funds might be negotiable CDs, brokered-insured deposits, federal funds, or reverse repos, for example.

The branch management can maximize profit by successfully marketing a large volume of deposits at a price that is below the cost of raising funds through alternative distribution channels. Because the cost savings may occur in the future, as in the case of longer-term deposits, we must take the present value of these interest savings. The present value of these cash flows is computed on all deposits new to the depository and on all deposits repriced during the period under analysis. The appropriate discount rate would be the firm's cost of capital (*coc*). Deposits such as demand deposits, money market demand accounts, and savings accounts are considered in this analysis to be repriced each day.

While we have chosen to reprice transaction and passbook accounts daily, alternative assumptions should be used based on the institution's experience. Many commercial banks, for example, have analyzed their transaction and passbook accounts and have concluded that an average effective maturity of from one to three years is a good approximation. Money market demand accounts have been estimated to have effective maturities from as short as thirty days to as long as ninety days or more at different institutions. If a longer maturity is used, then it is necessary to use an alternative funding source for yield comparison purposes that has the same longer maturity.

This analysis will produce the present value of the interest savings' cash flows ($PVIS$). To compute it, we take the difference between the interest rate on the alternative deposit source ($Ar_{i,t}$) and subtract the interest cost of the branch deposit interest rate ($Dr_{i,t}$). We then multiply this resulting interest spread by the amount of deposits of each type i originated or repriced by the branch during the current measurement period. We then take the present value, $Pv_{coc,t}$ of this series for cash flows over the number of periods the deposit is outstanding, t. We use the firm's weighted cost of capital coc as the discount rate. The weighted cost of capital assumed in our analysis is an arbitrary 9.00%. The firm with a pretax cost of equity of 25% and an average cost of liabilities of 7%, with a 6% equity ratio, would have a coc of approximately $\{[(25\% * 6\%) + (7\% * 94\%)] = \}$ 8.08%.

Table 8.1 shows an example of how data are organized to create the variables. The deposit cost data (DR) and (AR) must include the cost of deposit insurance, Regulation D reserves, and brokerage commissions, if applicable. It is important that the term structure of alternative funding sources be properly identified. They must represent the next-lowest cost of funding source for the institution. Do not use Treasury rates or rates that relate to another institution. These data need to be collected for each branch on an account-by-account basis. Most depositories have deposit account computer service systems that provide the data needed to complete the analysis. Once this is accomplished, the alternative funding source cost is compared to the interest cost of the new deposits and repriced deposits sold during the reference period, t. Sometimes it is necessary for institutions to make estimates of these interest spreads for large groups of similar deposits. This will generally provide satisfactory results.

Table 8.2 provides all the information necessary to calculate the present value of the interest savings on funds rolled over and brought in as new funds into a hypothetical branch for a one month period. To simplify the calculations without loss of accuracy, it is assumed that the interest savings on funds with maturities less than 30 days do not need to be discounted. It is also assumed all compounding is quarterly and that the interest savings' cash flows occur at the end of period t.

An example will help to illustrate how the calculations are made. Take the case of the one-year deposits. These funds will stay on account for one year and save the firm .25% as compared to the next-lowest cost one-year money. This

.25% translates into a quarterly positive cash flow of [(.25% /4) * $2,000,000] = $1,250 received at the end of each of the next four quarters. Discounting this quarterly savings at a weighted cost of capital of 9.00% gives $4,837.

Table 8.1
Example of Deposit Cost Comparisons
for All Deposits Sold by a Branch in One Month

Branch-generated deposit type	Rate: Dr_i	Alternative funding source	Rate: Ar_i	$Ar_i - Dr_i$
Demand deposits	0.00%	Federal funds	5.75%	5.75%
Savings accounts		Federal funds	5.75	1.50
	4.25			
3-12-month CDs		Negotiable 3-12-month CDs	8.58	.073
	7.85			
12-24-month CDs	8.24	12-24-month CDs	8.90	0.66

The value of the checking account deposits is determined by taking the interest savings of 5.75% for a month and multiplying it times the average weekly balance to get [(.0575/12) * $2,100,000 =] $10,063. The NOW account balances are handled in the same manner. It is necessary to identify the extraordinary marginal costs associated with transaction accounts such as checking, NOW, and MMDA. In this example, the depository has determined that the monthly cost of servicing these accounts is $3.50. The depository in our example has the following number and associated costs for these accounts:

Type of account	Number	Cost per month
Checking	1,800 accounts	$6,300
NOW accounts	1,200	4,200
MMDA accounts	800	2,800
Total costs per month		$13,300

Table 8.2 presents the present value of the interest cost savings resulting from the success of the branch in retaining repriced deposits and selling new deposits at interest rates below those paid on the next-lowest cost source of funds.

Branch fee and commission income (*BFC*) include fee income on transaction accounts of the branch, safety deposit box fees, ATM fees, checking account fees, and other fees earned. Commission income relates to products sold in the branch for which the firm receives commission for the availability of branch space, promotion, or direct sales effort by branch personnel. Table 8.3 provides an example of a hypothetical fee and commission schedule that might apply to a branch during a one-month period.

Branch total costs (*BTC*) include the direct costs of running the branch system, such as personnel, heat, light, space, telephone, mail, maintenance, and upkeep as well as all supervisory branch personnel, branch advertising, and branch back office costs. Many of these costs will be allocated on a per-account or per-employee basis. Branch space costs can best be uniformly estimated by charging the branch the rental cost at the current cost per square foot for commercial space in the locale of the branch. Otherwise, branch space costs could be unduly influenced by whether the firm owns the branch, or if rented, by when the lease was signed. These represent sunk costs or benefits. The problem of allocating occupancy costs was discussed fully in Chapter 4.

Table 8.2
Present Value of Interest Savings Calculated at the Firm's
Weighted Cost of Capital (9.00%) for all Deposits Rolled Over
and New Deposits Received for the Month of July 1996

Deposit type	*Amount of deposits rolled over or new*	*Term*	*Interest rate*	*Next lowest rate*	*Present value of interest savings @ 9%*
Checking	$2,100,000	Daily	0.00%	5.75%	$10,063
Negotiable order of withdrawal	$4,000,000	Daily	4.50	5.75	4,167
Money market demand accounts	4,800,000	90 days*	6.25	6.75	6,000
6-month CDs	14,000,000	6 months*	6.50	7.00	34,615
1-year CDs	2,000,000	1 year*	7.00	7.25	4,837
4-year CDs	2,000,000	4 year*	7.25	8.50	51,046
Total revenue from interest cost savings					$102,186
Less: Cost of transaction accounts					13,300
Total revenue after transaction account costs					$73,363

* 3-12 month accounts assumed to average 6 months, 12+ month accounts assumed to average 18 months.

Added to this must be the allocation of all indirect costs related to running the branch system. Allocations for data processing, human resource and training, communication, accounting, space management, and executive time must be included. These allocations, although admittedly difficult to obtain, as shown in Chapter 4, provide the necessary data to properly interpret the branch's profit performance. Typically, these allocated costs can be estimated quite accurately by making allocations on a per-account basis or per branch employee. An example of a schedule of total branch costs is shown in Table 8.4.

Table 8.3
Schedule of Fee and Commission Income
for a One-Month Period
(BFC)

Product type	Number sold	Compensation per unit sold	Income
Credit cards sold	23	$12	$276
Second mortgages	5	80	400
First mortgages	12	120	1,440
Safety deposit boxes	20	12	240
Checking fees received	120	6	720
Auto loans	12	25	300
Other loans	8	30	240
Annuities sold	10	80	800
Total fee and commission income *(BFC)*			$4,416

Table 8.4
Monthly Direct and Indirect Costs of Operating a Retail Branch
(BTC)

Heat, light, and rent	$15,200
Maintenance	1,290
Advertising and promotion	1,000
Staff costs plus benefits	8,765
Training and human resource allocation	765
Data processing allocation	32,453
All other allocations	12,776
Total costs *(BTC)*	$72,249

Table 8.5 provides a summary of each of the revenue and cost estimates assembled for the hypothetical branch. This branch was profitable during the month shown in the example.

It is now possible to determine the return on equity for the branch. Consider that the costs of closing the branch would involve 6 months of operating costs, which would cover severance, rental costs until the space is sublet, and other out-of-pocket costs. If this amount were $1,240,000, then the return on investment at this branch would be an annualized amount of (12 * $34,353 =) $412,236 of income divided by equity of $1,240,000, resulting in a return on equity of ($412,236/$1,240,000 =) 33.2%.

Table 8.5
Monthly Income Statement for Hypothetical Branch
(*TBP*)

Income:	
Deposit origination	$102,186
Fee income	4,416
Total income:	106,602
Costs:	
Direct and indirect	72,249
Income or (loss)	$34,353

BRANCH PROFITABILITY AND BEHAVIOR CHANGES

This branch profitability system is used in a growing number of institutions. The impact it has had on branch personnel behavior is sometimes profound. The model provides each branch with a monthly, or more frequent, profitability statement that allows it to measure its performance and compare it to that of other branches and to its own performance in previous periods. This is a powerful incentive tool. Consequently, the system is often used to develop branch manager incentive programs based on branch profitability. Using a system model has had the following advantages and disadvantages for supervising the personnel of depository branches.

ADVANTAGES

1. Branch personnel put their energy into selling those products that have the greatest profit reward (for example: branch personnel learn which CDs are the most profitable to the branch and develop sales methods to stress those accounts).

2. Branch personnel stress selling those products that have the best demand in their locale since profit is more important than some arbitrary target for cross-selling (for example: branches located far from auto dealers find that promotions of auto loans are not successful and they choose to stress other products in promotions).

3. Branch personnel become very concerned about direct expenses (for example: branch personnel stop using plant watering services to save money,

cut out subscriptions, and even share hotel rooms at branch managers' sales meetings).

4. Branch management becomes better at controlling head count (for example: branch managers quickly embrace the cost-saving's concept of using part-time help during peak periods).

5. Branch personnel are far less inclined to give away free services and wave service charges (for example: branch personnel don't go out of their way to tell customers about the highest interest rate account, often the least profitable to the branch, unless forced to sell it in order to retain the account);

6. Branches that have excess space are quickly identified and alternative locations or subdivision of the excessive space for alternative use becomes a goal (for example: branch personnel propose uses for unneeded space, including subletting or selling additional products).

7. Branch managers feel more in control and accountable with a profitability system they understand and can monitor (for example: managers develop a PC-based profit model to track branch sales and profits daily).

8. Branch managers who were trained in the "old school" of technical proficiency, as opposed to sales management, will be quickly weeded out by the "sales" pressure imposed by the branch performance system (for example: branch managers with strong technical skills voluntarily give up branch manager jobs in favor of becoming senior operating manager).

DISADVANTAGES

1. Using net profit to determine branch performance can be demoralizing to some staff. Some branches are simply not profitable, and there is little that can be done in the short run to change the situation. This can demoralize the personnel of those branches. One idea is to make a year-to-year change in profitability the goal.

2. Branch profitability can be shown to produce large fluctuations. One reality of branch profitability is its surprising volatility caused by the changing relationship (basis) between the interest rates paid by the branch for retail deposits and those paid for alternative wholesale sources of funds. During periods of rising market interest rates, the retail deposit rates tend to lag open-market rates, causing the branches to be very profitable. Just the opposite occurs during periods of declining open-market interest rates.

MANAGING A BRANCH WITH A PERSONAL COMPUTER

Once the firm has worked out its transfer prices for acting as agent, originator, and servicer, the branch can load the revenue for each product onto a personal computer and manage the branch daily using the sales statistics they produce. While each branch won't know exactly what each month's cost allocations will be, it can almost precisely calculate the revenue it generates from product sales of both assets and liabilities.

The hardest revenue item to compute is the present value revenue the branch receives from selling deposits, but generally someone in the asset/liability management department can provide that information each time deposit prices change. Then the new price can be loaded into the computer to determine that day's revenue. Once this is accomplished, the branch manager is in total control of monitoring and assessing the performance of the branch. Managers generally hold periodic staff meetings to go over recent sales and profit results and plan how to improve performance.

USING THE SYSTEM TO ANALYZE BRANCH PURCHASES, SALES, CLOSURES, AND SWAPS

This system is very successfully used for analyzing the profitability of branches available for purchase and for valuing existing branches for possible closure, sale, or swap. To use it, it is necessary to forecast expected average spreads between the rates paid on deposits attracted through the target branch and alternative funding sources. The target branch's expenses can usually be fairly estimated by using actual historical data. Then, a forecast of future deposit growth is made along with estimates of commission and fee income. By discounting these pro-forma cash flows over a five to ten year period, the analyst is able to determine the maximum deposit premium that might be offered to buy or a price to sell or swap a target branch.

The Resolution Trust Corporation was the largest seller of financial institution branches in recent years until its dissolution at year-end 1995. Its duties were taken over by the FDIC. These were branches of failed savings and loans. The largest numbers of acquisitions were known as purchase and assumptions in which deposits, certain other liabilities, and a portion of the assets are sold to acquirers. The largest numbers of acquirers of former S&L branches were commercial banks through July 1994. The greatest number of institutions were located in Texas. Other states with high branch sales included California, Louisiana, Illinois, and Florida.

Acquiring institutions paid an average premium of 3.11 percent of total core consumer deposits, excluding large denomination CDs and brokered accounts. This average premium probably underestimates branch values since a number of institutions sold valuable branches just prior to being seized by the RTC.

Using the branch performance system, it becomes very easy to determine which branches might be candidates for purchase or sale. It also makes very clear the special advantages of branch purchases that can be merged into an existing branch office. This situation provides a large increase in deposits, without a commensurate increase in costs. Branch swaps with other institutions that provide the same result for both parties are also very rewarding.

EXAMPLE OF BRANCH VALUATION

First Bank is considering bidding for a branch located across the street from one of its existing offices. By purchasing the branch from the FDIC, they can close it and shift the deposits to their existing branch without much increase in operating costs.

The branch for sale has deposits of $22 million. It has been declining in size since the FDIC took over management. If First Bank purchases the branch and assumes the deposits without assuming assets, it can repay some of its wholesale deposits and lower its cost of funds. However, it expects to lose deposits because of customer confusion about the closing of the branch and the firing of some personnel.

The president of First Bank has asked the head of retail banking and the financial officer to come up with a bid that will provide a solid profit. It is necessary to determine the net present value of the investment in the branch assuming a pretax weighted cost of capital to the bank of 10 percent. The two executives have come up with the following data for analysis. Table 8.6 shows the expected deposit balances for the next three years through 1996 and their best guess beyond 1996. It also shows the expected average spread between the cost of funds for the deposits purchased in the FDIC branch transaction and the expected cost of wholesale funds.

The revenue from additional fees and product sales from the new customers is assumed to be zero. The additional one-time and ongoing costs of the addition to their customer base of the $22,000,000 in deposits are also shown in the table.

Table 8.6
Estimated Deposit Balances and Average Spread Compared
to Wholesale Funding Source for 1993–1996 and Beyond
(dollars in millions)

Year	Average balance	Interest spread versus least cost alternative	Number of accounts
1992 (January)	$22	0.45%	5,200
1993	17	.040	4,500
1994	14	0.45	3,500
1995	12	0.50	3,300
1996–2001*	10	0.50	2,200

*No value ascribed to accounts after ten years.

The additional costs of servicing the additional accounts are shown in Table 8.7. Converting the account files to First Bank's computer system and notifying all the new customers also involve some major costs. These are shown in the table as well.

The cost of servicing accounts is estimated to be $12 per account per year.

In order to assess the value of this branch, a cash flow statement using the costs and revenues discussed is developed. The statement shows the cash outflows representing the conversion and one-time customer costs of assimilating the new deposits. Then the present value of the deposit cost savings less the servicing costs is calculated. The discount rate should be that of the firm's weighted cost of capital. For simplification, any value of the deposits after ten years is ignored. All cash flows are assumed to occur at the end of each year and taxes are ignored. The result of the analysis is the determination of the maximum discount First Bank can pay for the deposit base.

Table 8.7
Account Servicing and Conversion Costs

Costs of conversion	*Amount*
Computer conversion costs	$12,000
Moving file costs	5,000
Closing out and moving safe deposit boxes	5,000
Personnel costs during transition	5,000
Promotion and advertising	3,000
Total	$30,000

The objective is to determine the value of the new deposit base. This is determined by calculating the interest savings on the deposit base together with fees and subtracting the marginal operating and conversion costs. It is necessary to solve for the maximum deposit premium that can be paid, such that the present value of the interest savings on the new deposits for a ten year period discounted at a 10 percent cost of capital is equal to the transition costs plus the premium (the amount of the investment). This analysis is shown in Table 8.8.

Using this net present value analysis, the maximum value of this deposit base is only .5943% of the initial balance of $22,000,000. The bank would have to bid something less than .5943% for this transaction to be very profitable to the bank.

Table 8.8
Investment Analysis

Year-end Dec. 31	Revenue: Interest savings	Cost of servicing accounts	Net cash flows	Discounted cash flows @ 10%
1992	$99,000	$62,500	$36,000	$32,727
1993	68,000	54,000	34,000	28,099
1994	63,000	42,000	21,000	15,776
1995	60,000	39,600	20,400	13,933
1996	50,000	26,400	23,600	14,654
1997	50,000	26,400	23,600	13,322
1998	50,000	26,400	23,600	12,111
1999	50,000	26,400	23,600	11,010
2000	50,000	26,400	23,600	10,009
2001	50,000	26,400	23,600	9,099
Total				$160,740

$30,000 + Premium = $160,740
$160,740 - $ 30,000 = Premium = $ 130,740
Maximum premium percent = $130,740 / $22,000,000 = .5943%

SUMMARY

For most depositories, the objective of retail branch offices is to attract transaction and savings liabilities that are less costly than liabilities available in wholesale markets. Determining how well a branch accomplishes this task is not as easy at it appears.

The branch performance system described in this chapter is designed to evaluate the performance of retail deposit-gathering branches. The branch is credited for the present value savings of attracting deposits that are less costly than the next-lowest cost alternative funding source.

The role of branches in assisting in the origination of other assets is also included in the model. Using the model provides management with a periodic profit and loss statement for each branch.

The branch performance model is successfully used to value existing branches for purchase, sale, or trade.

NOTE

1. Norwest Corporation, *Norwest Corporation 1994 Annual Report*, p. 4.

Chapter 9 . . . .

Measuring Loan Origination Office Performance

INTRODUCTION

Loan origination offices are the easiest units for developing performance systems. Domestic mortgage origination, commercial loan production offices and international loan origination offices are the most common loan production offices, operated by depositories. Origination offices typically have clearly defined missions. This is because they specialize in one primary function, the origination of financial assets. These offices produce assets for the firm's own portfolio and also frequently sell loans in the secondary market.

There are two corporate objectives of these offices: (1) to originate loans at the lowest costs possible; and (2) to meet or exceed the underwriting standards established by the investors in those loans. This relatively simple charge makes it relatively easy to adapt the generalized origination model presented in Chapter 7. Developing a performance system for these offices to accomplish this is the purpose of this chapter.

DETERMINING REVENUES OF ORIGINATION UNITS

As discussed in Chapter 7, the biggest problem in establishing a profit and loss statement for a loan production office is identifying the revenues of the office. Many loans do not produce explicit fee revenue or, when they do, produce fees that are insufficient to cover the costs of the origination process. This is because the loans themselves have additional intrinsic value that is available only to the originators of them. That extra interest spread is an interest rate strip embedded in the interest rate earned on the loans, a portion of which is compensation for the originator and another portion compensation for servicing the loans. Determining the revenue items for the origination offices is the first order of business.

ORIGINATION AND PROCESSING FEES

The easiest revenues to identify in the origination process are explicit fees charged the borrower. These fees are limited to those charges levied to cover the costs of origination.

There are occasions when a borrower is permitted to "buy down" the interest rate by paying up-front points in excess of those charged to cover origination costs. These buy-down points are simply a loan discount that will be amortized into income over the expected life of the loan. These buy-down fees do not belong to the origination unit and should not be included as origination fee income. Fees related to loan commitments are another group of fees that should not be included as origination income. Commitment fees involve the firm accepting liquidity, interest rate, and credit quality risks borne by the portfolio manager and, therefore, should not be assigned as revenue to the origination units.

INTEREST SPREAD CONTRIBUTION

In addition to explicit fees, most originated loans earn a higher interest rate than comparable loans that might be available for purchase in the secondary market. This interest strip is compensation for the origination unit. The second source of income to the origination unit is the present value of the interest strip earned on the originated loans. If originated loans didn't earn this additional interest strip compared to loans purchased in the secondary market or from brokers, there would be no reason to originate the loans. In that case, management is advised to take a very careful look at the value of maintaining the origination unit.

Of course, loan origination is a cyclical activity. As a result, there will be times when just about every loan origination office will be unprofitable. Home mortgage lending is notoriously cyclical given the impact that a rise in market interest rates can have on mortgage refinances. During these periods volumes are down and frequently pricing is very competitive, which causes the value of the interest strip to decline as well.

During most periods, however, it is typical for an originated loan to provide a higher rate of interest, the amount of the interest strip. This should result in a loan whose interest rate is higher than that required by the investor, whether the investor is the originating firm's portfolio or a secondary market purchaser.

Consider the example of a "plain vanilla" secondary market qualifying home loan sold to Fannie Mae. Our hypothetical loan is originated with a coupon rate of 7.75 percent. The borrower pays an origination fee of 1% of the loan's principal balance and another $300 in "junk fees" (miscellaneous fees to cover other lender work). The loan is sold in the secondary market, assuming no change in market interest rates, at a coupon rate of (7.75% - 0.375% =) 7.375%. This leaves an interest rate strip of 0.375%. This interest strip can usually be sold as a servicing contract to a mortgage servicing company at a price, calculated as a present value, of 1.50 percent to 2.50% of the loan's principal value, depending on a number of factors such as loan size and size of downpayment. This means that to the origination unit the loan is worth 1% of principal plus $300 plus 1.50 to 2.5% of principal. For a $200,000 loan, the total value is shown in Equation 9.1.

Origination value $= (.01 * \$200,000 + \$300 + .015 - .0250 * \$200,000)$
                      $= \$5000 - \$7,300$ [9.1]

This value must cover all the costs of origination including operating the branch offices and the home office, where underwriting and documentation departments, shipping department, executive staff, and quality control unit are located. This value also assumes that the loan meets all established underwriting standards. Loans that cannot be sold to an investor become what's known as "lame loans" that are typically sold at lower prices.

How all this revenue gets split between the branches and the home office departments should be based on market indicators of the cost of origination. Fortunately, there are some good market indicators. In many markets loan brokers will sell loans or perform most of the functions of a loan origination office for a fixed percentage of the loan balance, say 1% to 1.5%. This market-established price gives the firm a good indication of the revenue to use as a transfer price for the origination offices. If these offices cannot originate at a lower cost, then their continued existence may not be justified.

The remainder of the revenue must go to pay all other costs of the mortgage origination unit. Table 9.1 shows an example of how the revenue might be divided between the various origination branches and home office departments for a product-line profit center originating 3,000 loans with a total principal of $450,000,000, an average balance of $150,000 using a value of the servicing spread of 2% of principal, an origination fee of 1%, and junk fees of $200 per loan.

DETERMINING COSTS OF ORIGINATION UNITS

Once the revenues are established, it is necessary to use the methods discussed in Chapter 4 to determine the direct and indirect costs of the mortgage origination unit. This is a rather straightforward process. Still, it is complicated by the need to identify indirect costs charged to the origination unit. Table 9.2 shows the income statements for the origination unit after these costs are identified.

Table 9.1
Mortgage Originator's Revenue

Type of revenue	Revenues	Loan origination of @ 1.25% of principal	Home office departments
Explicit origination fees @ 1% of principal	$4,500,000		
Junk fees @ $200 per loan	600,000		
Servicing spread @ 2% of principal	9,000,000		
Total revenue and allocations	$14,100,000	$5,625,000	$8,475,000 includes profit or loss

Table 9.2
Income Statement for Mortgage Origination Unit

Types of revenue and cost allocations	Loan origination unit: total revenues and costs	Loan origination office @ 1.25% of principal	Home office, shipping, etc.
Total revenue:	$14,100,000	$5,625,000	$8,475,000
Cost allocations:			
Indirect costs	1,625,000	125,000	1,500,000
Direct costs	12,075,000	5,925,000	6,150,000
Total costs	13,700,000	6,050,000	7,650,000
Profit or (loss)	$400,000	-$425,000	$825,000

Table 9.2 shows that the loan production office has experienced a loss and the home office a profit for the period in question. Similar statements are developed for such origination units as commercial business loans, credit cards, installment loans, and leasing units.

SUMMARY

This short chapter provides the basic performance system used to evaluate loan origination offices. This system is easier to implement than the performance system used for deposit-gathering branches.

The most difficult problem in implementing the origination performance system is determining the size of the interest rate spread (strip) to allocate to the origination units. This can be relatively simple in the case of loans with well-established secondary markets, such as mortgages, and difficult for commercial loans originated where no well established secondary markets exists. In those cases, estimates of the amount of the interest strip must be obtained by talking to security dealers and brokers who make markets in the loans in question.

Chapter 10. . . . .

Managing the Performance Measure Implementation Process

INTRODUCTION

The performance system implementation process involves a major commitment of the firm's senior management as well as from the accounting, data processing and profit center managers. Success comes only when senior management has a strong top-down commitment to performance measurement and a willingness to accept the inevitable internal friction and conflicts that result from the implementation process.

The implementation process begins with assigning responsibilities and pulling together the resources needed to complete the task. The organization issues raised in this process are the subject of this chapter.

PRODUCT-LINE REPORTING AND ORGANIZATION STRUCTURE

Make no mistake, product-line performance systems will shake up an organization. The CEO and/or President should serve on the steering committee for all but the largest institutions. These executives need to drive the process, demonstrate an understanding of it, and be alert to areas of extreme sensitivity. When managers first realize that they will be held accountable to an income statement, some will be threatened. For this reason, it is important that great care be taken in developing the organization structure used to plan and implement the product-line performance measurement systems.

There are two proven ways to successfully accomplish this task. The first is to assign someone who is not politically motivated. Most organizations have an individual who has no direct profit center responsibilities, is very respected in the organization, or is approaching retirement or has the trust of most of the organization. Such a person should have strong organizational and accounting skills and be sensitive to the firm's internal politics.

The second approach is to rely on outside consulting expertise. This is the most common method of dealing with highly charged and controversial issues such as the implementation of product-line performance systems.

PRODUCT-LINE REPORTING AND THE ACCOUNTING AND DATA-PROCESSING DEPARTMENTS

The accounting and data processing departments will be challenged by the development and ongoing operation of product-line performance systems. Both these groups always seem to have a full plate of user requests for new products, reports, and updated accounting requirements. Therefore, it is necessary to provide a dedicated group of accounting and data processing personnel who can command sufficient resources to keep the project moving forward.

Most of the information needed to develop product-line performance systems are already available. However, there are significant transformations of these data that have to be made to conform to the product-line reporting requirements. Most of these can be done off the mainframe using personal computers (PCs) with data downloaded from the central processor or a service bureau. This means that product-line performance reports can usually be accomplished without major software development. Off-the-shelf spreadsheet software is about all you need once the source data are identified and downloaded.

STAFFING NEEDS

The staff resources needed to accomplish product-line performance systems are directly related to the number of product-line origination, servicing, and brokerage units within the firm. A medium-size bank with ten or so product-line groups might need only 2 or 3 people working on the project for several months. A large, complex bank with 50 or more units might require three to five people for a year.

A large portion of the time associated with product-line reporting is to accomplish training. The systems used in this book are not well known by depository executives. They require looking at the firm's functions in new ways. It takes considerable training to help managers understand what they are being held accountable for and how their performance is to be measured.

The other big problem is allocating indirect expenses. There is no simple way to accomplish this task. Product-line managers know that indirect expenses have to be paid for, but they do not want their units to pay for them. They will fight hard to keep their allocations to a minimum. The process of making these allocations should take long enough to ensure each product-line manager that the process was deliberative, impartial, and as fair as possible. It takes considerable time to accomplish this result.

The overall implementation process is facilitated by setting up several single-purpose task forces. These include: (1) a senior management steering task force; (2) a management accounting cost allocation task force; (3) a data-processing task force; and (4) a shadow price task force. These groups can be augmented with outside consulting expertise if necessary. The functions of each task force are discussed below. Exhibit 10.1 provides a schematic showing the organizational staffing and reporting relationships for these task forces.

Exhibit 10.1
Organizational Staffing and Reporting Relationships

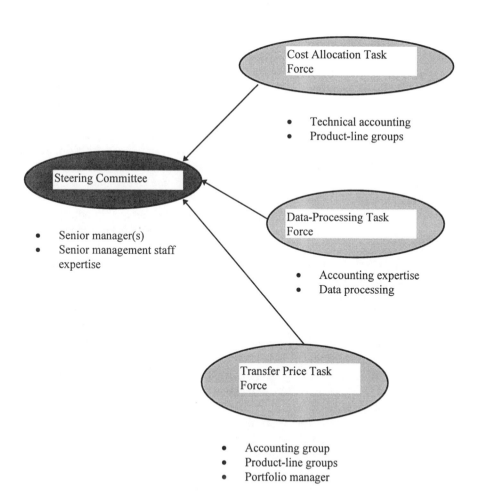

SENIOR MANAGEMENT STEERING TASK FORCE

Senior management drives the implementation process. If this group is not behind the project, then it is doomed to failure and becomes a costly, worthless exercise. This task force:

- determines which units within the firm are to be treated as stand-alone product-line profit centers
- develops a time schedule for accomplishing the task
- assures that product-line managers don't impede the process
- acts as arbitrator when conflicts arise concerning pricing and cost allocations
- assures sufficient resources are available to accomplish implementation

MANAGEMENT COST ACCOUNTING ALLOCATION TASK FORCE

The management cost accounting allocation task force has the difficult job of allocating the costs and revenues of the firm to each product-line profit center. This is both the hardest-working and most controversial task force. Assigning costs is not an easy job and will meet with considerable resistance. Consequently, this task force's chairperson should be above politics and considered a technician with an in-depth understanding of the firm. It is not important that the chairperson be of high rank; indeed, it's probably better if this person is not. It would be unwise to have managers think that there is intimidation at this stage of the process. Cost allocations will inevitably affect performance evaluations of personnel, so it is vital that each product-line profit center's managers know that the cost allocations were done as scientifically and fairly as possible.

This task force should also include a member of the accounting staff and should have a call on senior executives who can resolve disputes. Each executive in charge of indirect costs is asked to develop a supporting document that allocates the unit's costs to each of the product-line profit centers based on a consistent classification system. These schedules normally use time allocations (e.g., such as the training department), project costing (e.g., such as systems development costs incurred by the data processing department), allocation by number of employees (e.g., such as a payroll department), number of accounts (e.g., such as ongoing data processing costs incurred by the data-processing department), or number of employees assigned to accomplish a profit center's work (e.g., such as certain costs incurred by the accounting department). In many cases, combinations of the above classifications are used to make the proper allocations. After they work with these indirect expense allocations, it will not be long before the staff support areas act as if they are third-party providers of their service. Once they do so, they can bill the product-line profit centers for work performed by their unit. Table 10.1 provides several classification approaches for allocating support staff expenses for indirect cost allocating.

Table 10.1
Classification Approaches to Indirect Cost Allocations

Staff support unit	Typical approach to cost allocation
Accounting	Use time sheets
Data processing:	
Development work	Project costing
Ongoing processing	Allocate by CPU usage, disk megabyte use, tape mounts and usage, or pages printed
Human resources	Allocate by number of employees
Legal	Project costing by hour charges
Payroll	Allocate by number of employees
Planning	Project costing (as an internal consultant)
Training	Project costing (as an internal consultant)
Executive staff and board of directors	Use time allocation

The managers of each product-line profit center must also participate in the process. These managers will rarely agree with the cost allocations developed by the staff departments, thinking their allocations too high, but they should be satisfied that the process of allocation was fair and equitable. In order to achieve this result, these managers have to have a chance to challenge the allocations made by each indirect cost center. When necessary, these managers should be able to seek arbitration from a higher authority.

DATA-PROCESSING TASK FORCE

A data-processing task force is charged with determining how to download relevant information from a mainframe or from vendor-supplied systems needed for the product-line performance systems. This task force can be chaired by anyone having an overview of the data processing systems used by the firm and types of data found on them. Such a person is likely to be from the accounting or data processing department. Extracting data from existing systems and then using it for input into specialized PC-based performance measurement data-processing systems is typically the most effective way to manage the product-line performance systems.

The primary data required for input into the various performance systems include

- data on direct fees charged customers for various products and services

- dollar volume and number of financial products sold per time period on the asset and liability side of the balance sheet (these data are partially found in a typical detailed cash flow statement)
- direct expenses by product-line units
- indirect expense allocations by product-line units
- interest income and expense by type of asset and liability

There are a number of vendors who offer off-the-shelf performance management systems. Unfortunately, these systems do not use the same conceptual design as those recommended in this book. Consequently, it is generally not possible to adopt these systems. Rather, it is best to identify the data needed and use spreadsheet-trained analysts to develop the systems recommended.

TRANSFER PRICE TASK FORCE

The function of the transfer price task force is to determine the prices to be charged by the origination and servicing units for the activities they perform on behalf of the portfolio manager. This task force should be chaired by a senior staff person, possibly the same person who sits on the steering committee. There will also be need for expertise to collect data on third-party market pricing for origination and servicing services available from third parties.

The principal activity of the transfer price task force involves making significant decisions which ultimately make or break the performance of each origination and servicing unit. Most of these origination and servicing units do not receive origination or servicing fees explicitly from the borrower or the firm's portfolio. This makes it necessary to determine appropriate transfer prices to charge the firm's portfolio. For loans sold in the secondary market, origination and servicing revenues are explicit.

The transfer prices established must reflect as close as possible the prices that are charged to the portfolio manager to obtain these services from an independent third-party provider of these origination and servicing services. For many loans, these prices are available by surveying prices of third-party providers, e.g., mortgage servicing, some commercial loan servicing, auto loan servicing, and credit card servicing. For other products, especially liability products, efforts should be made to obtain comparable costs from peers or considering the cost of brokered deposits. Data from trade associations, consultants, or federal banking agencies can be useful.

PITFALLS

Management must prepare to address difficult issues that normally arise whenever major change is introduced into the organization. Make no mistake, the implementation of the recommended performance system will be viewed as a threat by many. Efforts will be made to discredit the systems. Recognizing this fact, it is important to anticipate potential problems and plan ahead how to deal with each. A number of common pitfalls of the implementation process are discussed below.

MANAGERIAL BEHAVIOR CHANGES

Experience has shown that for most depositories the implementation of the systems described in this book will lead to significant changes in employee behavior. Some units, especially those experiencing high profitability, will welcome the systems and then will expect to be financially rewarded for their exceptional performance. Others, especially those showing a loss, will feel threatened and be concerned about job security. Still others will reject the systems as irrelevant or faulty.

Senior management must prepare for each of these behavioral responses. Senior management must also expect to be surprised by the performance results. Some units thought to be marginal may turn out to be potential "home runs" for the organization in the years ahead. Other units thought to be the backbone of the firm may be found to be marginally profitable or even losers.

Given the threatening potential of performance systems in general, it is valuable to introduce the systems gradually. A two-to-three-month period should be devoted to a "test drive" during which system finetuning takes place. During this period, product-line profit center managers will learn what factors drive their performance, have a chance to challenge prices and costs thought to be incorrect, and, most importantly, have a chance to get an early look at what the performance of their unit is likely to be. This normally spurs groups with poor performance into action even before senior management intervention.

COST ALLOCATION CONFLICTS

Probably the greatest source of complaints by product-line profit centers is the indirect cost allocations. The best way to justify the indirect cost allocations is have the staff support areas that incur the costs develop a detailed schedule of their proposed allocations.

This may seem like a lot of unnecessary work, however, in the long run it will pay off. Ultimately the product-line profit centers will begin to explore outside third-party vendors for the services they obtain internally. They will argue that they can receive the same or better services for less cost. The internal support areas must anticipate this and be ready to justify the quality and cost of the services they provide. As they do, they will start acting as if they face competition, a not altogether unfortunate response.

Despite every effort to anticipate problems, conflicts over costs are inevitable. These must be resolved by a senior officer, the president in some cases, or the senior steering committee. Arguments over whether having inside staff support units or using outsider vendors is the way to go will also have to be resolved in the same way.

DATA AND MODEL CREDIBILITY

Some product-line profit center managers, facing unpleasant performance evaluations, will argue that the model is deficient and the data not credible. These problems are best overcome by intensive training in a nonthreatening atmosphere. These sessions usually take considerable time and require trainers who really understand the conceptual and technical aspects of the performance systems.

Since the performance systems are based on theoretically sound concepts of the functions performed by depositories, most managers will eventually understand the systems and appreciate the fact that they measure those activities over which the product-line managers truly have control.

Once their model's validity is established, the only arguments will be over cost allocations and prices received for origination and servicing functions performed. Managers should be encouraged to seek out market prices that might differ from those established internally so they can be investigated. The more information about proper transfer prices, the better the systems will be.

DEALING WITH UNITS EXPERIENCING LOSSES: MARGINAL PROFIT CONTRIBUTION

One of the biggest problems is the product-line profit center that is losing money. It's rare that all the firm's branches, origination, and servicing units are profitable. Staff working in those that are losing money will immediately conclude that their job is at risk. This means that senior management must prepare to move quickly if chances of salvaging the unit are dim. In other cases, the unit is expected to be able to improve its performance or may be suffering a temporary cyclical or seasonal downturn. These situations can be handled by having product-line managers draw up plans for improved performance and identify the factors that are giving rise to their problems. This process must, however, involve more than arguing that cost allocations are too high or transfer prices too low.

The performance system for deposit-gathering branches will permit management to rank the success of each branch in the system. For depositories with large branch systems this ranking process will likely identify a number of branches that do not achieve adequate profitability. These branches should be targeted for merging with an existing branch, a move to a better location, a sale, or a purchase of a competitor's branch to combine the two. In one institution that used the model, the firm had a policy that every year the management would implement a strategy to improve the performance of the bottom 10 percent of all their branches. Usually this involved purchases, trades, or sales.

In other cases, senior management determines that they are willing to accept losses in a unit for some extended period of time if the unit is covering its marginal costs. If the firm cannot cut indirect costs with the elimination of the unit, then the fact that the unit covers its direct marginal costs is of some short-term benefit. Nevertheless, these units must eventually solve their performance problems.

UNTIMELY REPORTS (INFREQUENT OR EXCESSIVE LAGS IN REPORTING)

Just as good board members expect to receive accurate and timely management reports, it makes no sense to implement an elaborate product-line performance system if the product-line managers do not get accurate and timely reports. In today's competitive atmosphere, quick, intelligent decisions determine success or failure.

One test of senior management's commitment to product-line performance systems is that they devote enough resources to making sure the reports are available soon after the reporting period closes.

MEASURING QUALITY

The biggest problem with any internal transfer system is evaluating quality of services performed. The portfolio manager pays the origination and servicing units for services performed. These prices are based on a basic definition of the quality of services to be performed. The origination units are assumed to be underwriting and documenting the loans and accounts they create according to the agreed-upon criteria negotiated with the portfolio manager. There will inevitably be disagreements over the quality of services provided.

One way to address quality issues is to provide for periodic audits of the various units that provide these functions. The internal audit department can evaluate the quality of origination and servicing services in relation to the terms established. Issues such as adequacy of loan documentation, delinquency rates, loan losses, and other statistics must be assessed periodically to determine the quality of services obtained.

Assessing the quality of service provided by staff support units is much more difficult. How does one easily assess the quality of accounting, legal work, or data processing? There is no simple answer to this question. Ultimately, however, the users of the services must be given a chance to evaluate the services they obtain in light of the transfer costs they are allocated. This process will turn up staff support areas in which the general consensus will be that the quality of the services does not measure up to the costs. These support units will have to address their weaknesses, personnel will have to be changed, or the services obtained externally.

SUMMARY

The commitment of senior management to performance measurement is essential if the organizational upheaval caused by the introduction of these systems is to be worthwhile. There are many problems involved in introducing these systems into an organization. Most of them can be anticipated and dealt with effectively. The most difficult problem is the product-line profit center or staff support area that is performing below par. These shortcomings cannot be ignored since these weaknesses will quickly be widely known throughout the organization. Consequently, senior management must be prepared to act quickly when they learn bad news.

Chapter 11 . . . .

Measuring Performance of Local Promotion and Advertising Programs

INTRODUCTION

This chapter describes how to create systems to evaluate the performance of local promotion and advertising programs used by deposit-gathering branches to increase sales of products and services. The purpose of this performance system, called the Locally Executed Advertising and Promotion (LEAP), is to bring focus and accountability to an area of corporate expense that is usually not effectively assessed.

As more depositories adopt the notion that deposit-gathering branches are really financial product and service retail distribution centers, the need increases to provide branch sales managers with tools designed to raise sales. One such method is to allow these branch personnel to develop local area promotions or advertising programs designed to leverage off of the branch staff's knowledge of the local market they serve.

The performance system described here has been implemented in just about every competitive setting, from branches that serve neighborhoods of large metropolitan areas to those serving small rural towns.

WHY THE LOCAL PROMOTION?

The ongoing consolidation of the depository industry is making it essential that branches be given greater latitude in marketing their products and services. As large institutions merge and operate over large geographical areas, the need for local autonomy in marketing and promotion grows. Without this discretion, the smaller, locally based institutions will be able to attack the out-of-state institution as a "carpetbagger" having little knowledge of and concern for the local community. This can only be countered if the branch management is sensitive to local customer needs and has the capability to meet local needs by implementing quality promotions that have pinpoint timing and utilize themes that define the branch as having sensitivity to the community.

Smaller institutions also need the ability to respond to local needs quickly. Local branches need to be able to deploy promotions that can be rolled out quickly to respond to competitors' programs. Indeed, it is this ability to respond effectively to local needs that may be the smaller institutions' salvation in the years ahead.

DEFINING THE LOCAL PROMOTION

Promotions can be defined as a special activity designed to accomplish a specific objective during a limited period of time. Promotions may offer the customer a special price, but in all cases offer an immediate customer benefit of some kind. Promotion differs from normal marketing activities such as media advertising, public relations, and customer referrals, although these typical marketing activities might be employed during a promotion. Promotions can be designed to stimulate a specified customer response or a desirable employee behavior.

Promotions are part of the overall marketing strategy of the firm and should be programmed as part of the firm's overall marketing planning process. They should also advance the overall positioning and image of the branch and firm and reflect the character of the branch. Promotions should be carefully thought out and organized.

FIVE BASIC PREPROMOTION STEPS

There are five important steps that should be accomplished before any promotion takes place. These include: (1) complete an internal analysis of your customers; (2) analyze the branchs existing customer base; (3) analyze the branch's market area; (4) analyze the competition; and (5) determine the branch's image. These are discussed below.

Complete an Internal Business Analysis

Before launching any promotion, it is essential to have a record of existing customer cross-sell ratios, sales of existing products, and the profitability of every product. It does not make sense to promote products that lose money for the firm. Thus, this performance system cannot be used until the branch performance system in Chapter 8 has been implemented.

Analyze Your Customers

You should know the characteristics of your core customers, those customers that provide 75 percent of your business in terms of demographics and psychographics. What do your customers need? When are they likely to need it? In Northern climates, home improvement loans are not likely to draw a response in January.

Analyze Your Market

Keep in mind the simple axiom that in most cases 80% of your customers live or work within a three-minute or three mile radius from your office. By identifying major retail, office, and factory complexes, the potential customer identification job is made easy. It is also necessary to get more specific by identifying hospitals, large employers, civic buildings, clubs, schools, and other potential targets of promotions.

Analyze Your Competition

It is necessary to know your competition. Who are your primary and secondary competitors? What is the focus of their marketing programs? What are the advantages and disadvantages of their product and service offering compared to yours? This assessment must be done objectively. If you competitors have a more convenient location, more parking, or a larger office, maybe you can counter with shorter lines.

Determine Your Image

Using a variety of techniques, it is important to know your branch's image. What do customers and noncustomers think about you? Some firms use mystery shoppers or focus groups to learn this. Others simply have employees talk to friends about what they think and compare notes.

THE OBJECTIVES OF PROMOTIONS

The nine primary objectives of promotions include:

1. To encourage trial of your branch among noncustomers and former customers.
2. To stimulate repeat business from present customers and build customer loyalty.
3. To increase business activity during specific hours, days of the week, or times of the month.
4. To increase transaction activity through cross-selling.
5. To introduce a new product.

6.   To help offset competitive advantages or activities of competitors, to take the focus off the competition, and to focus on your office.
7.   To capitalize on holidays, seasons, or special events (such as community celebrations).
8.   To create an event that adds excitement to your branch several times a years. Your customer should enjoy promotions and like the extra activity associated with them – simply for their entertainment value.
9.   To stimulate employee enthusiasm and involvement. When consumer promotions are properly presented to employees, they almost always have this important side effect.

THE PROMOTION PLANNING PROCESS

Promotion planning is a four-step process, including: (1) promotion preplanning; (2) establishing the promotion's objectives; (3) developing a specific promotion plan; and (4) obtaining staff involvement and enthusiasm.

PROMOTION PREPLANNING

Promotion preplanning involves assessing the past record of your branch and its competitors in running promotions. Your experience and that of your competitors provides significant clues as to the potential success or failure of a promotion. To accomplish this preplanning the following questions should be answered:

* Which promotions have we had in the past that have been successful and unsuccessful?
* What are the factors that contributed to the past promotions' success or failure?
* Which promotions can simply be replicated?
* What can be done to turn failures and marginally successful promotions into successes?
* What promotions have competitors run and how do you assess their success?

ESTABLISHING THE PROMOTION OBJECTIVES

At this point it is necessary to identify the planned promotion's objective. This objective will be taken from the list of objectives discussed above. Of course, it is likely that the promotion will have multiple objectives. Eventually, these objectives must be made very specific in terms of new product and service sales.

Branch promotions should represent a profitable use of firm funds. Whether a promotion is financially successful is ascertained by completing the "Return on Promotion Investment" (ROPI) analysis shown in Exhibit 11.1. The purpose of the ROPI is to provide a simple structure for collecting and analyzing data that bear on the success or failure of a promotion. The analysis requires that the promotion planners specifically forecast the sales expectations for the planned promotion. To accomplish this analysis, it is necessary to identify the products involved in the promotion forecast, the sales of the product generated by the promotion, and the profit per unit of sale. These data allow you to forecast the profits generated by the promotion. The next step is to estimate costs. One of these costs is the cost of providing a lower price or special offer. Dividing the profits generated by the cost provides the simple-to-use index ROPI. An index over 1.0 indicates the promotion covers its cost. Below 1.0, the promotion does not cover costs, and if management goes ahead with it, they must use other than purely financial criteria to support it.

Exhibit 11.1
Return on Promotion Investment

SALES FORECAST			
Product(s)	Profitability per unit (a)	Sales in units (b)	Profit (a * b)
Product #1			$
Product #2			
Product #3			
TOTAL REVENUE			$
PROMOTION COSTS:			
Newspaper			
Direct mailing and printing			
Mailing list			
Flyers, banners, and posters			
Premiums/giveaways			
Special pricing			
Other marketing costs			
TOTAL PROMOTION COSTS			(B) $
ESTIMATED ROPI			(A ÷ B) $

The ROPI system can be used to develop a simple break-even analysis for the promotion. By changing the expected product sales volume, it is possible to determine the minimum number of sales needed to equal costs, and therefore, determine the promotion's breakeven point. That is the quantity of sales generated by the promotion that will exactly cover all the promotion's costs.

The ROPI can be used after the promotion is completed to evaluate its success or failure.

DEVELOPING A SPECIFIC PROMOTION PLAN

Developing a specific promotion execution plan involves establishing schedules for development of promotion materials, running ads, staff training, production of banners, and all the other hundreds of details that determine the difference between success and failure. Exhibit 11.2 provides a form that can be used to systematically plan the execution of a promotion.

Exhibit 11.2
Promotion Plan

1. PRODUCT GOALS

Product(s)	# Product sales	Total # of sales

2. TARGET MARKET

[ ] Existing customers   [ ] Noncustomers
Demographics:
[ ] Combined household income level: $_____
[ ] City and/or zip or census tracts: _____
[ ] Age range: _____
[ ] Homeowners/ renters: _____
[ ] Employer targets: _____
[ ] Other target characteristics: _____
Competitive Advantage/ Benefit/ Special Factors:
[ ] Competitive prices: _____
[ ] Special fee/ service charges: _____
[ ] Quick processing: _____
[ ] Unique product feature: _____
[ ] Special event: _____

3. MEDIA PLAN

Point-of-sale materials:
•   Posters
•   Banners
•   Buttons
•   Flyers
•   Counter cards/ tent cards
•   Other
Print ads:
Publication: _____Frequency:
_____

Insertion dates: _____
Direct mail:
Target list
Telemarketing:
- In branch
- Script writing requirements
- Prospect list
Exhibit:
- Trade show booth
- Umbrella stand
- Local merchant exhibit
Publicity and community relations:
- Press release
- Charitable contribution
- Other
Premium traffic builders

Keep in mind that there are few innovations in promotions. It's not surprising that thousands of promotions are concentrated around back-to-school, holidays, vacation time, seasons of the year, and local celebrations.

OBTAINING STAFF INVOLVEMENT AND ENTHUSIASM

Your staff is key to successful promotions. They should be involved in the planning process. If the staff does not feel good about the promotion, they will either not sell it, or worse, will make fun of the process. Good training should make the staff comfortable that they are selling something that is "good" for the customers they see every week. Some steps that might contribute to success include:

- Hold a staff rally.
- Provide a staff incentive (group or individual).
- Request feedback during and after the promotion.

Another way to improve the chance of success is to develop an implementation guide for the staff. This guide should be available several weeks before the promotion and should include:

- objectives and goals
- dates
- materials
- instructions for implementation
- responsibilities of various staff members
- measurement techniques (how to measure success)

The execution process can be improved by using a promotion timeline. This report, shown in Exhibit 11.3, provides a simple way to describe:

- what needs to be done
- how it is going to be done
- who is responsible
- when it needs to be done

Exhibit 11.3
Promotion Timeline Report

Activity	How to accomplish	Person responsible	Date due

PROMOTION RISKS AND DANGERS

Most promotions can be expected to enhance the branches' image and contribute positively to overall positioning in the market. However, there are a number of dangers inherent in various types of promotions that should be considered:

- too many discount-oriented promotions can adversely affect market image
- couponing too frequently tends to made people wait for the next one before buying
- premiums are a big risk when you have to commit to buy merchandise in volume. Many issues are involved. Is the premium timely? Will it catch on?

SUMMARY

Promotions are one of the most effective means to improve branch office performance and involve employees in the process in a way that can build teams and job satisfaction. A number of steps can be taken to improve chances of success:

- Set specific realistic objectives.
- Evaluate costs and determine the promotion's profitability.
- Implement the prepromotion steps.
- Target the customers for the promotions.
- Involve and include staff in promotion planning.
- Develop a specific realistic timetable for implementation.
- Track the results of the promotion and review performance of promotions.

Chapter 12. . . . .

Cost Cutting with Product-Line Systems

INTRODUCTION

The product-line performance systems developed in previous chapters are powerful tools for implementing cost-cutting strategies at depositories. The key to successful cost cutting is giving managers the tools to tell them how well they are performing so that decisions can be made to reduce or discontinue ineffective activities and to stress or expand profitable ones. This assessment is easier with product-line systems.

These product-line systems also provide the impetus for rationalizing and improving the effectiveness of staff support units. Once each product-line profit center is periodically charged for the services of each staff support unit, pressures will build to reduce their costs.

This chapter describes the use of product-line systems for supporting cost-cutting strategies.

PRODUCT-LINE SYSTEMS HELP DECIDE BUSINESS STRATEGY

The basic strategic value of the product-line systems for evaluating origination, servicing, and brokerage units is to develop the firm's long-term strategy for the future. Most depositories developed many new products and services during the highly competitive period of deregulation in the 1980s. The problem for many firms is that many unprofitable products and services continue to be offered even though the firm may face weak demand, excessive competition, or lack necessary economies of scale.

The product-line systems described in Chapter 7 allow senior management to assess each operating unit's performance. Those that are not profitable can be eliminated, or necessary changes in personnel, product design, pricing, or marketing strategies can be implemented in hopes that the unit can achieve profitability. Experience shows that most firms have several units that are unlikely to achieve acceptable results in the near future.

Senior management typically has inadequate resources to spend trying to turn around every subperforming unit. That means some of the units must be eliminated. This is done by shutting down the unit and, if possible, selling the portfolio of loans together with servicing to another firm. Alternatively, the firm might choose to continue to offer a product, but act as a broker-agent for another firm that specializes in it. In the future, smaller depositories can expect to become distributors of products for larger firms that can support the origination and servicing of complicated financial products. These firms will develop strategies to make use of their customer relationships to sell a greater number of products, including those the firms cannot produce on their own.

Larger institutions might take just the opposite approach. These firms will identify areas where they enjoy economies of scale or a technological advantage over the competition. They will market higher volumes through agents rather than invest more resources in brick and mortar to originate the product.

SETTING COST GOALS

For depositories using aggregate measures of performance such as those discussed in Chapter 5, the job of setting goals for cost cutting can be very difficult. This is because there is no objective standard for evaluating whether a particular line of business has high or low costs and productivity.

Quite the opposite is the case using the product-line performance systems described in this book. Each of the systems produces easy-to-understand profit-and-loss statements that can be compared to those of specialized competitors. These systems provide for the assigning of equity capital to each unit so that return on equity measures is computed and evaluated against all the other product-line operating units in the firm.

These performance systems give senior management the tools they need to evaluate operating performance throughout the firm. They also allow comparisons across different types of functions, such as origination and servicing. Units not achieving the firm's target profit or return on equity targets are easily identified so that remedial work can be done on them.

PRODUCT-LINE SYSTEMS HELP DECIDE WHETHER TO DO-IT-YOURSELF

The product-line systems of Chapter 7 also permit senior management to identify operations best done by third-party vendors. Specialists in origination and servicing exist for virtually every major asset product offered by depositories. This means that management can use product-line systems to identify operations that might best be contracted out to third parties.

The opposite is also true. Some firms might develop especially effective origination or servicing capabilities in a specified asset. This asset is a candidate for expansion through secondary market sales and servicing for others. Most large-sized firms have strategies to originate home mortgages for sale into the secondary market in order to generate origination and servicing income. However, there are many more opportunities available. Credit cards, mobile home loans, auto loans, and large corporate loans are suitable for secondary market operations.

Alternatively, some firms have a very strong retail market franchise in a particular geographical area. This means a firm could serve as an effective broker-agent for other firms that have a weak consumer franchise in their market. This allows the firm with the strong customer base to offer a broader array of products without attempting to operate origination and servicing units.

PRODUCT-LINE SYSTEMS ASSIST IN COMPANY-WIDE COST CUTTING

Product-line systems allow senior management to delegate many more decisions to the managers of product-line profit centers. Senior management retains the ability to control using its product-line performance reports. However, with product-line performance systems and consistent compensation systems, the product-line managers have the incentive to find cost-cutting opportunities wherever they are within their units.

Product-line managers launch their cost-cutting efforts in a number of ways. First, they challenge their indirect cost allocations. This is covered in the next section. The second way is to assess their own operations. This is generally a welcome and productive activity. Almost any product-line unit can find ways to improve productivity, reduce waste, and better rationalize the product line. Usually this process is left to the product-line managers to plan and implement on their own.

Cost cutting is tougher to deal with when it involves benefits required by the "corporate office." Vacation time, benefits, and working hours are typically determined by a centralized staff unit on a company-wide basis. These are typically offered universally throughout the organization. Sometimes, however, a product-line unit will be up against competitors that specialize in one product and enjoy lower personnel costs or space costs. This leaves only two alternatives. Allow the unit to reduce personnel and space costs to industry norms or, alternatively, handicap the unit by allowing it to continue to pay higher costs. Eventually, the first approach must be taken since no product-line unit can be expected to prosper indefinitely if it has a noncompetitive cost structure.

PRODUCT-LINE SYSTEMS HELP REDUCE STAFF SUPPORT COSTS

Challenging indirect cost allocations is usually a constructive process. Managers of the indirect cost centers generally respond to pressures by product-line managers by reviewing all their services and sitting down with product-line managers to determine whether the services provided are needed and cost effective. Too many times the indirect staff support areas provide the product-line managers what "they" think these units need. Often, however, these services are not as important to the product-line managers as the staff support units believe. The process of reviewing the services and the costs of providing them is extremely worthwhile and usually leads to lower costs.

Unfortunately, this process can also be potentially destructive if the process gets out of hand. In the extreme, the product-line profit centers will seek to control as much in the way of staff support activity as possible, thinking they can get more responsive services at a lower price. At times, this is true. When a staff support unit devotes the vast majority of its output to support one product-line unit, then it may make sense to transfer oversight of the unit to that product-line unit.

At other times, the cost-challenge process results in the product-line support units becoming involved in destructive arguments over the costs and quality of services provided. This is particularly true for staff units that are hard to assess, such as data processing and accounting. Ultimately, senior management has to decide whether the costs and services provided by these units are cost effective and make their decision known to the product-line units that must pay for them.

PRODUCT-LINE SYSTEMS HELP REDUCE EMPLOYEE HEADCOUNT AND COSTS

Another advantage of product-line performance systems is that they frequently result in the recognition that personnel costs are high and in need of control. Product-line managers will be quick to point out what they consider to be excessive staffing levels in staff support areas. As discussed in the previous section, these challenges must be allowed to take place.

In addition, senior management and the human resource department must be prepared to offer suggestions and provide the tools needed to facilitate staff reductions in the product-line units as well. One of the most effective means for reductions is using part-time personnel. The product-line deposit-gathering branch performance system gives the managers a strong incentive to replace full-time personnel with lower-cost part-time people. This process is facilitated if the human resource group has a plan ready to go. Once the branch managers see how part-time personnel can reduce costs, they generally become willing users of the program.

Larger servicing units are also motivated to lower personnel and space costs by moving facilities to lower-cost cities and metropolitan areas. Many New York City-based institutions have moved processing units to New Jersey. In recent years, some California-based firms have moved processing units to such places as Las Vegas to reduce costs.

LOCAL AREA PROMOTIONS AND ADVERTISING SYSTEM RATIONALIZES MARKETING COSTS

Most marketing people do not naturally look at their activities in the same way the finance person might, as an investment designed to produce a return. Marketing people are more concerned with image, demographics, psychographics, media, message, and a whole host of other qualitative factors that are anathema to the quantitative finance types. The finance person, relying on return-on-investment models, is concerned about cash outflows and inflows related to marketing and promotion expenditures. As shown in Chapter 11, the two approaches are not necessarily incompatible. The trick is to introduce the system described in Chapter 11 and let the situation take care of itself.

In one institution in which the promotion and advertising system described in Chapter 11 was implemented, expenditures on advertising and promotion fell shortly after implementation. This was not, as you might suspect, because the effort to do the analysis was too rigorous, rather it was because the branch personnel found that too many of their promotions were ineffective. Many found that simple promotions such as large, colorful banners, in-branch brochures, and simple customer referral programs could produce the highest return for the investment dollar.

SUMMARY

Product-line performance systems are valuable tools for the implementation of cost-cutting programs at depositories. The systems provide both the stimulus for cost cutting and the information needed to assess the desirability of various cost-cutting programs.

The beauty of the performance evaluation systems outlined in this book is that they all use standard performance measures such as net profit and loss and return on equity to evaluate performance. These are measures familiar to all business managers. They make it easy to set profitability goals and to measure performance against them.

Selected Bibliography

Aggregated Thrift Financial Report. Office of Thrift Supervision. Annual.

Allan, Franklin. "Information Contracting in Financial Markets." In Bhattacharya, Sudipto, and George M. Constantinides, eds. *Financial Markets and Incomplete Information.* Savage, MD: Rowman and Littlefield, 1989.

Annual Statistical Digest. Board of Governors of the Federal Reserve System, Washington, D.C.

Baron, D. P., and B. Holmstrom. "The Investment Banking Contract for New Issues under Asymmetric Information: Delegation and the Incentive Problem." *Journal of Finance,* (December 1980): 1115–58.

Benston, George J., and Clifford W. Smith, Jr. "The Transaction Cost Approach to the Theory of Financial Intermediation." *Journal of Finance,* (May 1976): 215–33.

Bradley, M.D., and D. W. Jansen. "Deposit Market Deregulation and Interest Rates." *Southern Economic Journal,* (Oct. 1986): 478–89.

Brewer, Elijah, III, Diana Fortier, and Christine Pavel. "Bank Risk from Nonbank Activities," *Economic Perspectives* (Federal Reserve Bank of Chicago), July/August 1990.

Burns, Merrill O. "The Future of Correspondent Banking." *Magazine of Bank Administration,* (May 1986).

Cherin, A. C., and R. W. Melicher. "Branch Banking and Loan Portfolio Risk Relationships," *Review of Business and Economic Research,* (Sept. 1987): 1–13.

Davenport, T. O. and H. D. Sherman. "Measuring Branch Profitability," *Banker's Magazine,* (Sept.–Oct. 1987): 34–38.

Davis, R., L. Korobow, and J. Wenninger. "Bankers on Pricing Consumer Deposits," *Quarterly Review Federal Reserve Bank of New York,* (Winter 1987): 6–13.

Davis, R. and Korobow, L. "The Pricing of Consumer Deposit Products—The Non-rate Dimensions," *Quarterly Review Federal Reserve Bank of New York*, (Winter 197): 14–18.

Diamond, Douglas. "Financial Intermediation and Delegated Monitoring." *Review of Economic Studies*, 51 (1984): 393–414.

————. "Asset Services and Financial Intermediation." In Bhattacharya, Sudipto, and George M. Constantinides, eds. *Financial Markets and Incomplete Information*. Savage, MD: Rowman and Littlefield, 1989.

Ernst & Young, LLP, *Performance Measurement for Financial Institutions*, Chicago: Richard D. Irwin, Inc. 1995.

Fama, Eugene. "Banking in the Theory of Finance." *Journal of Monetary Economics* (1980): 39–57.

Faust, W. H., "The Branch as a Retail Outlet," *Bankers Magazine*, 173 (Jan.-Feb. 1990): 30–35.

Hirtle, Beverly. "The Growth of the Financial Guarantee Market." *Quarterly Review Federal Reserve Bank of New York*, Spring 1987).

Jilk, L. T., "Strategies for Pricing Core Loans and Deposits." *Bankers Magazine*, 171(Nov.-Dec. 1988): 47–52.

————. "Branch Banking and Risk." *Journal of Financial and Quantitative Analysis*, (Mar. 1968): 97–108.

Roosevelt, Phil. "Fee-Income Boom of the Eighties Cools Off." *American Banker*, (January 7, 1991).

Sealey, C. W., Jr. "Valuation, Capital Structure, and Shareholder Unanimity for Depository Financial Intermediaries." *Journal of Finance* (June 1983): 857–71.

Shafton, Robert M., and Donald D. Gabay. "The Banking Outlook for Diversification into Insurance." *Bankers Magazine*, (Jan./Feb. 1985).

Statistics on Banking. Federal Deposit Insurance Corporation, Washington, D.C. Annual.

Thygerson, Kenneth J. *Financial Markets and Institutions*. New York: HarperCollins College Publishers, 1993.

————. *Management of Financial Institutions*. New York: HarperCollins College Publishers, 1995.

————. "Modeling Branch Profitability." *Journal of Retail Banking*, (Fall 1991): 19–24.

————. "A Product Line Performance Appraisal System for Financial Institutions," *The Community Banker*, (Fourth Quarter 1995).

Index

arbitrage, 19
asset and liability transformations, 16
asset-backed security, 6,7
asset credit quality, 59
asset/liability committee, 9, 16
ATM, 9, 42, 82, 104

bank holding company (BHC), 79
Bank Insurance Fund, 2, 57
Board of Governors, 70
brokerage, 20, 23–24, 90
brokered deposits, 7
branch origination income, 101–102
branch servicing income, 101
branch total costs, 101, 105
break-even, 133

capital adequacy, 52, 57–58
capital adequacy ratio, 52, 58
channel of distribution, 20
Chase Manhattan, 6
combined analysis, 48
common-size financial statement, 47
core deposits, 65–66
correspondent services, 82
covenant, 20, 23
credit risk, 16

credit risk reports, 22
credit risk transformations, 17
cross-sectional analysis, 48, 49
cross selling, 77
currency transformation, 17
customer group, 40
cybernet, 1

data-processing task force, 121, 123–124
default risk cost, 42
denomination transformation, 16
document control, 20

economies of scale, 11, 12, 77, 78
equity multiplier, 58
expense allocation model, 37–40

Fannie Mae, 1, 89,114
FDIC, 97, 109, 110
Federal Financial Institutions Examination
      Council, 70
federal funds, 7
Federal Reserve Board, 79
Federal Reserve's Regulation Q, 5
financial claim/function matrix, 25–31
financial leverage, 52, 57–59
financial ratios, 49, 52–70

Financial Standards Accounting Board, 52
foreclosures, 21, 60
fully allocated costs, 38–39

GAAP, 2, 70, 78, 85, 93
government sponsored enterprises, 74
guarantees, 19, 83

information processing, 20, 78
interest rate risk, 16, 36, 62–63

liquidity, 19
loan commitment, 20
loan disbursement, 20
loan loss provision, 61–62
loan monitoring, 20
Locally Executed Advertising
    and Promotion, 129
location, 41
loss leader, 5, 6

management accounting cost
    marginal contribution, 37
marketability transformations, 17
maturity transformation, 16
medium of exchange, 18
Money Store, 24
monitoring, 24
mortgage bankers, 24

net interest margin, 55–56
net interest spread, 55–56
New York Stock Exchange, 24
nonbank, 74
noninterest, 73–84
noninterest expense, 69
noninterest income, 52, 54, 73–84
nonperforming loans, 62
note issuance facility, 83

off–balance sheet, 12, 28, 52
operating efficiency, 67–69
operating expenses, 68
operating risk, 57
organizational division, 40
origination, 20, 57, 86, 113–117
overcollateralization, 17

participation, 81, 86
past-due payments, 22
performance reporting system, 35–45
periodic GAP, 63–64
portfolio income, 90–91
portfolio management, 36
portfolio risk management, 18, 19
product-line manager, 119
product-line performance system, 6, 35, 93

real estate appraisal, 79
Regulation Q, 5
repossession, 21, 60
Resolution Trust Corporation, 98, 109
return on assets, 54–55
return on equity, 48–49, 53–54, 57
return on promotional investment, 132–133

Sallie Mae, 1
Savings and Loan Insurance Fund, 2
secondary market, 6, 81
securitization, 17
senior management steering
    task force, 121–122
servicing, 20, 21, 22, 57
servicing reports, 19
shadow price task force, 121, 124
Sheshunoff & Co., 70
SNL Securities, L.P., 70
standby letter of credit, 67, 83
Statement of Financial Institution
    Standards, 65
Statistics on Banking, 70
strategic planning, 32
swaps, 83, 110
syndication, 19, 81, 86

time-series analysis, 48–49
transfer price task force, 121, 124
trust services, 80

unallocated expenses, 38
unbunding, 2, 15, 34, 85
Uniform Bank Performance, 70

wholesale distribution channels, 65

About the Author

KENNETH J. THYGERSON is Professor of Finance at California State University, San Bernardino and Principal in KTV Associates, a financial institutions consulting firm. Previously, he was CEO and President of the Federal Home Loan Mortgage Corporation and several other public companies, Chief Economist of a national trade association, and a member of President Reagan's Commission on Housing. He is author of *Financial Markets and Institutions: A Managerial Approach* (1993), *Controlling Corporate Legal Costs: Negotiation and ADR Techniques for Executives* (Quorum 1994), *Management of Financial Institutions* (1995), and *The Financial Institutions Internet Sourcebook* (1997).

ISBN 1-56720-104-0